NATURAL BOR

NATURAL BORN KILLERS
Quentin Tarantino

faber and faber
LONDON · BOSTON

First published in 1995
by Faber and Faber limited
3 Queen Square London WC1N 3AU

Photoset by Parker Typesetting Service, Leicester
Printed in England by Clays Ltd, St Ives plc

© Quentin Tarantino, 1995

A CIP record for this book
is available from the British Library

ISBN 0-571-17617-8

2 4 6 8 10 9 7 5 3 1

Natural Born Killers

INT. COFFEE SHOP – DAY

A coffee shop somewhere in New Mexico. Mickey Knox, his back turned to us, is sitting at the counter finishing a meal. We hear the ping . . . bang . . . of a pinball machine being played off-screen.

Mabel, a waitress, comes over and fills Mickey's coffee cup.

> MICKEY
>
> What kind of pies do you have?

> MABEL
>
> Apple, pecan, cherry, and key lime.

> MICKEY
>
> Which do you recommend?

> MABEL
>
> Well, the key lime is great, but it's an acquired taste.

> MICKEY
>
> I haven't had key lime pie in ten years.

> MABEL
>
> When ya had it, did ya like it?

> MICKEY
>
> No, but that don't mean much. I was a completely different person ten years ago. Let's give key lime a day in court. And a very large glass of milk.

Mabel turns to her right.

> MABEL
> (*to someone off screen*)
> Should I make that two pieces?

Camera pulls back and we see for the first time Mallory Knox, Mickey's wife, sitting on a counter stool next to him. Her back is to the camera as well.

3

MALLORY

Nada, Rosey.

MABEL
(*annoyed*)

My name's not Rosey.

(*points at name tag*)

It's Mabel.

MALLORY

Whatever.

Mabel exits frame.

Mallory gets up from the stool, walks over and grabs the Jerry's kids' can next to the cash register, then dumps out the coins on the counter and selects a quarter.

MABEL

Hey, what the hell do you think you're doin'?

Mallory saunters past the Cowboy playing pinball. As his eyes follow Mallory, he loses his ball.

She walks to the jukebox in the back, inserts the quarter, selects a song, punches the buttons, a needle lands on a record, and a good God almighty rockabilly tune cuts through the coffee shop.

Mabel brings Mickey his pie and milk.

MABEL
(*to Mickey*)

She ought not be doing that. That's for Jerry's kids, not rock 'n' roll.

Camera moves around to a close-up of Mickey. This is the first time we see him. As he takes a bite of green pie:

MICKEY

I can't take her anywhere.

Mallory starts doing a slow, seductive fandango around the coffee shop. She's really cooking and smoking.

Pinball Cowboy and Mabel are starting to wonder just who the hell these people are.

4

Mickey isn't paying much attention. He's too busy enjoying his pie and milk.

EXT. COFFEE SHOP – DAY

A dirty pickup truck, sporting a Confederate flag decal, pulls up to the coffee shop. Sonny, Otis, and Earl, three tough-looking rednecks, pile out. Steam rises from beneath the pickup's hood.

> EARL
> Goddamn, this sumbitch is runnin' hot. Y'all go inside. I'm gonna check 'er out.

INT. COFFEE SHOP – DAY

The loudness of the rockabilly song slaps Sonny and Otis in the face as they walk inside the door. The sexy sight of Mallory doing the ubang stomp stops them in their tracks.

> SONNY
> Good God almighty, what the hell is that?

> OTIS
> That's a bitch outta hell, son.

Otis and Sonny exchange looks.

> SONNY
> Take a run at 'er, kiddo.

Otis heads toward Mallory. Sonny moves over to the counter next to Mickey.

> Miller, Mabel.

> MABEL
> Comin' up.

Otis stands in front of Mallory, trying to copy what she's doing. Her eyes are closed at the moment, so she doesn't see him.

Mabel sets the Miller down in front of Sonny. Sonny takes a swig, enjoying the floor show.

SONNY
(*to Mickey*)
That's some sweet piece of meat, ain't it?

Mickey turns from his pie and looks at Sonny. His expression betrays nothing.

The needle lifts off the record. The song ends.

Mallory opens her eyes and sees Otis. Otis gives her his best shit-eating grin.

Mallory punches Otis hard in the face, spinning him around.

Sonny spews out a mouthful of Miller Highlife.

Mallory grabs the back of his head and smashes his face twice down on the table.

Otis buckles, dropping to his knees.

Sonny jumps off the counter stool, but Mickey's hand clutches hold of his shoulder.

Sonny spins around toward Mickey, loaded for bear, and points his finger at him, threateningly.

Before any threat can be made, Mickey whips a large buck knife out from its sheath and, in a flash, slices off Sonny's finger.

Sonny's finger drops on his boot. He grabs his aching hand. Blood spurts out of the stub in the rhythm of a pulse . . . one . . . two . . . spurt . . . three . . . four . . . spurt . . .

MICKEY
Just because my woman's mopping up the floor with your buddy is no reason for you to join in.

Mickey makes five lightning-quick slashing swings. The buck knife slips back into its sheath. At first, there seems to be no difference with Sonny. Finally, blood flows from the slices made in his face and chest. Sonny collapses.

The Short-Order Cook charges out of the kitchen at Mickey, wielding a meat cleaver and screaming.

Mickey whips out a .45 automatic from a shoulder holster inside his jacket and fires.

CU of bullet flying through the air.

Bullet's POV: Heading fast toward Short-Order Cook's face. It hits. Short-Order Cook puts his hands to his face and falls to the ground, screaming.

Mickey spots Earl, who's standing outside the plate-glass window. Earl's watched the whole shebang.

Earl mouths 'Fuck!' He turns and runs for it.

Mickey hurls the knife through the plate-glass window, which shatters. The knife plunges deep into Earl's back. He hits the ground dead.

Mickey turns to Mallory. She's sitting on top of Otis pummeling him with punches.

Honey.

Mallory looks up at Mickey. She gets off Otis and moves to Mickey's side.

Mickey trains his .45 on Pinball Cowboy, who's shaking in his cowboy boots. Mickey aims at Mabel, who's clutching her coffee pot, crying.

(*to Mallory*)

Pick one.

Mallory does eanie, meanie, minie, mo, pointing back and forth from Mabel to Pinball Cowboy.

MALLORY

Eanie, meanie, minie, mo, catch a redneck by the toe. If he hollars, let him go. Eanie, meanie, minie, mo. My mom told me to pick the best one and you are it.

She ends, pointing at Mabel. Mabel's crying. She screams:

MABEL

NO!

Mickey fires the .45. The bullet chinks through the coffee pot Mabel's holding and explodes, thunking her in the chest. She hits the floor, dead.

7

Mickey and Mallory join hands and walk over to the Pinball Cowboy.

MALLORY

When you tell people what went on here, tell 'em Mickey and Mallory Knox did this. Understand?

Pinball Cowboy nods yes.

The two killers plant a big wet kiss on each other's mouths. Then, holding hands, Mickey and Mallory walk out of the café.

CREDIT SEQUENCE:

INT. COUPE DE VILLE – MOVING – DAY

Mickey and Mallory in a flashy '68 Cadillac Coupe de Ville. Duane Eddy's 'Rebel Rouser' blares on the soundtrack. The background is an outrageous process shot. The titles splash over this image, 50s-style.

When this sequence is over, we cut to black.

END CREDIT SEQUENCE

Over black screen, we hear:

CAPTAIN SQUERI

Send Scagnetti in here.

INT. POLICE STATION – SQUERI'S OFFICE – DAY

Camera is positioned in the middle of the office. The door is in the middle of the frame.

Jack Scagnetti flings the door open and steps inside Squeri's office. Squeri's never seen.

SCAGNETTI

You wanted to see me, Capt'n?

CAPTAIN SQUERI
(*off*)

Scagnetti, go up to interrogation room C. Dewight McClusky, chairman of the prison board, is waiting to meet you. You're

8

gonna deliver two prisoners from the county jail to Nystrom
Insane Asylum in Bakersfield.

SCAGNETTI

This is bullshit. I'm a detective. You want an errand boy, call
Jerry Jewis.

*Scagnetti spins around and leaves the room, slamming the door shut
behind him. Captain Squeri shouts after him.*

CAPTAIN SQUERI
(*off*)

Not this time, Jack!

INT. POLICE STATION CORRIDOR – DAY

*Police Detective Scagnetti walks rapidly down the hallway, wearing an
old, wrinkly, black suit jacket.*

*People walk by in the foreground and background. Scagnetti slips an
already tied tie over his head.*

INT. INTERROGATION ROOM C – DAY

*Dewight McClusky, a man in his fifties, wearing a business suit, stands
in the foreground reading a book with his back to the door. In the
background, Scagnetti enters the room.*

SCAGNETTI
Jack Scagnetti. You wanted to see me?

McClusky turns toward Scagnetti.

MCCLUSKY
Congratulations on the Curtis Fox case, Scagnetti. You put an end
to a nightmare. The ladies of this city can get to sleep again, and
they have you to thank.

SCAGNETTI
Thank you, sir.

Warden Dewight McClusky of the California Prison Board. Take a seat, please.

Scagnetti lowers into a chair in front of the interrogation table.

(*referring to book*)

This is damn good reading. I'm surprised Hollywood hasn't found you. This would make a better movie than that *Serpico* shit.

McClusky puts the book down, we see the title: Curtis Fox: The Capture and Death of a Serial Killer. *Author Jack Scagnetti. McClusky sits on the edge of the table, facing Scagnetti. He lifts a file off the table, then tosses it in Scagnetti's lap.*

I think you'll find that good reading as well. Mickey and Mallory's file. You familiar with them?

Scagnetti opens it. It's the files, reports, and photographs of Mickey and Mallory Knox. Scagnetti's face lights up.

SCAGNETTI

Who isn't?

MCCLUSKY

You been followin' the news coverage?

SCAGNETTI

They've been separated since their incarceration in a couple of penitentiaries –

MCCLUSKY

Susanville, Soledade.

SCAGNETTI

They've killed a shitload of inmates and guards –

MCCLUSKY

Five inmates, eight guards and one psychiatrist all in one year's time . . . Very good. You keep up with the headlines.

Scagnetti nods.

Our situation in a nutshell is . . . no prison wants 'em, no prison will take 'em. I'm even talkin' about fuckin' hellholes, where the warden's as hard as a bar of iron. No one wants those fuckin' assholes behind their walls, dealin' with 'em day in, day out.

SCAGNETTI

I can appreciate that.

MCCLUSKY

So can we. So the solution to our little problem is we had them deemed crazy. And we're shippin' 'em to Nystrom Asylum for the Criminally Insane.

SCAGNETTI

Lobotomy Bay?

MCCLUSKY

You've heard of it?

SCAGNETTI

So, how do I fit into this scheme?

MCCLUSKY

The public loves you, Jack . . . You don't mind if I call you Jack, do you?

SCAGNETTI

By all means.

MCCLUSKY

You're a celebrated cop. Twenty-six years on the force, a bestseller out in paperback . . .

McClusky grabs Scagnetti's book and reads from the back cover.

'A modern-day Pat Garret. A hell-bent lawman with a deadly axe to grind with maniacs.'

McClusky lowers the book.

You're a breathing icon to the old style of justice; eye for eye, tooth for tooth. Ya know what I mean.

Scagnetti nods.

That's why you've been the lucky boy chosen to deliver Mr and Mrs Knox. We, the prison board, know that once you get them on the road if anything should happen, an escape attempt, an accident, a fire, anything . . . that Jack 'Supercop' Scagnetti would be there to look out for his public's best interests.

SCAGNETTI

I see.

MCCLUSKY

You write the script, Jack. Call it, whatever, '*Showdown in Mohave: The death of Mickey and Mallory.*' Have we found our man?

SCAGNETTI

You found him.

INT. COUNTY JAIL – CELL BLOCK CORRIDOR – DAY

Scagnetti's POV: McClusky stands next to a big iron door. He bangs on it with his fist. We stay on Scagnetti's POV through this scene.

MCCLUSKY

Pete, open it up! I'm comin' through with a visitor!

A buzzer sounds.

McClusky opens the door and we follow him down the corridor. As soon as the door opens, we can hear a female voice singing the song 'Long Time Woman.' McClusky turns to Scagnetti as they walk.

Well, Jack, I'll tell ya, in all my years with the penal institution, and I'll tell ya that's no small number, Mickey and Mallory Knox are without a doubt the most twisted, depraved group of fucks it's ever been my displeasure to lay my eyes on. I mean, those two rat shits are a walkin' reminder of just how fucked up our system really is.

The song 'Long Time Woman' is getting louder as they proceed.

SCAGNETTI
(*off*)

Who's the song bird?

MCCLUSKY

Mickey's better half herself, Mallory Knox. This little lady drowned her father in a fish tank.

INT. A LIVING ROOM – NIGHT

CU of a home aquarium with fish swimming around. Suddenly, Mallory's father's head is shoved into the tank.

BACK TO: PRISON CORRIDOR

MCCLUSKY
While the two together burned her mother alive in her bed.

INT. A BEDROOM – NIGHT

Medium CU of Mallory's mother lying asleep in bed, mouth open. What looks like a gaz nozzle appears at the top of the frame, pouring gasoline all over her face. She coughs and gags. Camera pans up and we see Mickey holding a gas can.

CU of Mallory with a lit match by her face. She tosses it in front of her. We hear the sounds of Mallory's mother igniting.

BACK TO: PRISON CORRIDOR

MCCLUSKY
They blew up the fucking house along with half the block.

INT. MICKEY AND MALLORY'S CAR – MOVING – NIGHT

Process shot: Mickey behind the wheel, Mallory in the passenger seat. They kiss, as we see the house explode in the background.

BACK TO: PRISON CORRIDOR

Still Scagnetti's POV:

SCAGNETTI
(*off*)
Why?

McClusky's still walking ahead of us.

MCCLUSKY
Because they wouldn't give them their blessing for marriage.

SCAGNETTI
(*off*)

Ain't love grand?

McClusky laughs.

MCCLUSKY
Ain't love grand? That's a good one.

Still Scagnetti's POV: We look down from McClusky to Mallory's file in his hands. It contains her picture and lists her color of hair, color of eyes, height, weight, race, etc. Beneath that is a column which reads: Psychiatric Remarks.

As we read the remarks, we hear a Psychiatrist's voice read aloud.

FEMALE PSYCHIATRIST
(*voiceover*)
When pressed about the reason for the murders . . . patient became hostile . . .

INT. A PSYCHIATRIST'S OFFICE – DAY

Looking trashy, wild, and animalistic, Mallory's a sex-machine dressed in a prison gown. She sits in a chair, looking directly at the camera.

MALLORY
I don't owe you a explanation! I don't owe you shit! I'm not here for your entertainment. If I don't tell you what you wanna hear, what are you gonna do? Throw me in jail? I'm already there, you stupid pigfucker. You gonna give me some more time? I've already got life. What else you got to threaten me with? Death? I'd like to see you fuckin' try. I haven't met one motherfucker here who's shown me shit!

BACK TO: DEATH ROW CORRIDOR

Still on Scagnetti's POV:

We look up from the file and see McClusky's leaning against a cell door.

We hear somebody singing 'Long Time Woman' inside the cell.

We move to McClusky, who, looking into the camera, gestures toward the cell.

MCCLUSKY

Here she is . . . you know her, you love her, you can't live without her . . . Mallory Knox.

We pan from McClusky to the inside of the cell where we see Mallory, her back to us, singing and dancing.

INT. PRISON – MALLORY KNOX'S CELL – DAY

CU of Mallory's face singing 'Long Time Woman.'

MALLORY
(*singing*)

Ninety-nine years is a long, long time. Look at me, I will never be free, I'm a long time woman . . .

MCCLUSKY
(*off*)

Hey, Knox! Somebody out here wants to meet you.

Mallory just keeps on truckin'.

MALLORY
(*singing*)

Been workin' on the road now.
Been workin' by the sea.
Been workin' in the cane fields,
and I wanna be free . . .

Mallory's POV: We stare at McClusky and Scagnetti for a second. Then, like a bull, we charge/dolly straight at them. Mallory screams out of shot. We smash head-first into the bars. Mallory's POV flings up, looking at the ceiling, then falls backward.

Medium tight shot of floor, Mallory falls into frame, out cold.

CU on Scagnetti through the cell bars.

SCAGNETTI

Jesus Christ!

Camera pans over to close-up on McClusky.

15

MCCLUSKY

Don't worry about it. She does that all the time.

BACK TO:

Mallory on the floor, still unconscious, with blood trickling down her scalp.

MCCLUSKY
(off)

Follow me.

INT. PRISON – LONG CORRIDOR – DAY

Camera is at the end of a long corridor. McClusky and Scagnetti approach from the other end. Scagnetti's studying the files.

Phil Wurlitzer comes up behind the two men.

WURLITZER

You duckin' me, Dewight?

MCCLUSKY

Hey, Phil, how the hell are ya?

WURLITZER
(to Scagnetti)

This son of a bitch is chairman of the prison board, but it's like pullin' teeth to get him down to a prison.

MCCLUSKY

Why would I want to fuck around at a prison? The only reason I'm here now is to set him straight, and I'm on the next flight out.
(to Scagnetti)
Jack, this is the superintendent of the jail, Phil Wurlitzer. He's the man who's got the power of the pen here.

Wurlitzer shakes hands with Scagnetti.

WURLITZER

Pleased to meet ya, Jack. I read your book. I'm impressed. Good work on Curtis Fox.

SCAGNETTI

Thanks.

MCCLUSKY

From now on, you'll be dealin' with Phil. He can answer all the questions you got about the arrangements. I'm gonna be bidding you good luck and ado in about twenty minutes. My flight back to Sacramento leaves LAX in a hour.

WURLITZER

And I want you to know, we'll all cry a river when you're gone.

They all laugh.

SCAGNETTI

What's the traveling arrangements?

WURLITZER

Well, Mickey and Mallory can't be together. So, we'll put you on one of our prison busses and you'll take Mallory first, then you'll come back for Mickey.

SCAGNETTI

And where do you keep Mickey?

WURLITZER

We got his stinkin' ass in the deepest, darkest cell in the whole place. But it just so happens that right now he's got a special visitor.

SCAGNETTI

Who?

WURLITZER

Wayne Gayle.

SCAGNETTI
(*surprised*)

Wayne Gayle!

INT. JAIL – VISITING AREA – DAY

Wayne Gayle, a young, energetic, commando journalist à la Geraldo Rivera, is sitting on the visitor side of the county jail visiting area. Wayne

17

is alone and the visiting area is empty. Apparently, some arrangement was made for the visit. Wayne has a miniature tape recorder in his hand and is testing it.

> WAYNE
> (*into recorder*)
>
> Testing one . . . two . . . three . . . testing . . . one . . . three . . . over, over, over, Mickey Knox meeting.

Wayne shuts off the recorder, rewinds and plays it back. It works beautifully. He hits the record button and conceals the recorder in his sports coat pocket.

The door opens on the prisoner side and Mickey Knox is led into the room by two Sheriff's Deputies. Mickey's wearing the county jail blue jumpsuit. He has a thick, wide leather belt around his waist with a metal ring built into each side. Long sturdy chains with handcuffs on each end are wrapped across his body and through the rings, binding his arms to his sides. His hands and feet are double-cuffed.

The Deputies both have their guns drawn, ready to blow Mickey in half at the slightest provocation. For a man wrapped and bound in chains, Mickey seems strangely in control of his environment. Restrained as he is by the symbols of society (the chains, jail, guards, guns, jumpsuit), he remains a dangerous, intimidating, and fascinating figure.

Wayne takes in the image of Mickey.

> WAYNE
> (*to himself*)

Showtime.

Mickey's roughly shoved into his seat on the prisoner's side of the glass. The Deputies move to their place, off to the side by the wall.

> Hello, Mickey. We've never been introduced, but I'm Wayne Gayle. I'm a journalist on television. I don't know if you've ever heard of me or remember me. I was one of the reporters outside the courthouse during your trial –

> MICKEY

Everybody knows who you are. You're famous.

Wayne pauses and retorts.

                    WAYNE
I could say the same thing about you.

                    MICKEY
                    (*smiles*)
Ya sure could.

                    WAYNE
I want to thank you very much for seeing me.

Mickey is silent.

I have a television show. It's very popular. Every week we do a
profile on a different serial killer. You don't mind if I call you a
serial killer, do you?

Mickey shakes his head.

The episode we did on Mickey and Mallory was one of our most
popular ones.

                    MICKEY
Did you ever do one on Wayne Gacy?

                    WAYNE
Yes.

                    MICKEY
Whose ratings were higher?

                    WAYNE
Yours.

                    MICKEY
How 'bout Ted Bundy? Ever do one on him?

                    WAYNE
Yes. Yours got the larger Nielson share.

                    MICKEY
Good . . . yuppie piece of shit.

                    WAYNE
What I'd like to do –

MICKEY
How 'bout Manson?

WAYNE
Manson beat you.

MICKEY
Yeah, it's pretty hard to beat the king.

WAYNE
We've been waiting to do a follow-up episode on you for a long time. And that time has definitely come.
(*pause*)
I feel it's apparent to anyone who's hip to what's going on that the prison board has thrown the constitution straight out the fuckin' window. You and Mallory may be killers, but you're not insane. You belong in a prison, not an asylum. The prison board is blatantly railroading you into a hospital for the sole purpose of turning you into vegetables. Now some people are saying, 'So what?' I am not one of those people. If we avert our eyes while they do this to you, we give them permission to do it again whenever they see fit. Today they wipe clean your mind because they feel your actions are dangerous, tomorrow they wipe clean my mind because they feel what I say is dangerous. Where does it all stop?

No response from Mickey.

My problem, Mickey, is that you don't exactly inspire empathy. I'm all alone on this. I need your help. I want what the prison board is doing to be the focus of our follow-up episode. Now I have interviews with chairman of the prison board, Dewight McClusky, about this issue. And I'm tellin' ya, Mickey, he looks bad. The two psychologists they used for their psychiatric kangaroo court won't talk to us, which always looks bad. I have an interview with both the judge of your trial, Burt Steinsma, and the psychologist and author, Emil Reinghold, both of whom discount the notion that you're insane.

You put that all together, and what the state is doing becomes obvious. But the network isn't satisfied. They feel the show needs another element. It needs you. In order to put the show on the air,

I need to get an interview with you. You haven't talked to the press since your trial. Now, a few days before you get transferred to an asylum, you grant an interview on television with Wayne Gayle. We're talkin' a media event here. Every son of a bitch out there with a TV set's gonna tune in to see that. We'll make their motives so blatant, we'll shame 'em into dropping the whole thing. At least for a little while, the publicity would keep them from just giving you and Mallory lobotomies. Well, whatta ya say?

MICKEY

Have you talked to Mallory about this?

WAYNE

She won't even see me, Mickey. Now you're not supposed to know anything about what's going on with her, but I'm gonna tell ya somethin'. Since you two've been sentenced, Mallory hasn't spoken one word.

MICKEY

She doesn't talk?

WAYNE

Not to anybody. She sings.

MICKEY

She sings? What does she sing?

WAYNE

Songs. 'He's a Rebel,' 'Leader of the Pack,' 'Town Without Pity,' that Dusty Springfield song 'I Only Want to Be with You.' That's what I hear, anyway. Her behavior was the main thing the doctors' report used against you. So even if she would see me, which she won't, I couldn't put her on camera anyway. If I ask her, 'Mallory, are you insane?' And she starts singing 'Dead Skunk in the Middle of the Road,' that blows our whole case.

Mickey cracks a smile.

The guards come over to take him away.

DEPUTY SHERIFF
(*off*)

Time, motherfucker!

They grab Mickey hard, then jerk him out of the chair.

> WAYNE
> Wait a minute, Mickey, I need an answer.

Mickey doesn't respond. He just leaves with the guards.

> *(yells after him)*
> Just think about it. But don't think too long.

INT. MICKEY'S CELL – DAY

Medium CU of Mickey curled up by his bed, writing Mallory a letter.

> MICKEY
> *(voiceover)*
> Dearest Mallory. My cell is so cold. At night I get the chills. I pretend you're lying next to me, holding me from behind with your leg draped over mine and your arms wrapped tightly around me. I lie in my cell . . .

DISSOLVE TO:

Wide shot in cell behind Mickey. We slowly dolly back.

> *(voiceover)*
> . . . and imagine kissing you. Not making love, just kissing for hours and hours on end. I remember everything about our time. I remember every joke you ever told.

CU of the letter being written over the wide shot.

> I remember every secret you ever shared. Shared or revealed? I think shared is proper. I remember every single time you laughed.

Extreme CU of Mickey, mouthing the words as he writes. We can hear Mallory's laugh – a distant haunting echo.

> I remember every meal we ever ate. I remember your cooking. I especially remember your casseroles. I remember watching *David Letterman*.

We hear the echo of television laughter.

I remember driving fast . . . faster, man, fast behind the wheel of the Coupe de Ville.

The sound of the Coupe de Ville swells until we . . .

CUT TO:

EXT. COUPE DE VILLE – NIGHT

Camera sits on the hood looking down at Mickey and Mallory, driving fast – slow motion. A hurricane of wind whips through their hair. Mallory laughs wildly as she wraps her arms around Mickey and kisses.

MICKEY
(*voiceover*)

You, baby, by my side. Your bare feet up on the dash, singing along with the radio 'Needles and Pins,' 'He's a Rebel,' 'You're My World,' 'Ring of Fire,' 'Love Grows Where My Rosemary Goes,' 'Groove Me' . . .

DISSOLVE TO:

EXT. COUPE DE VILLE – NIGHT

Coupe de Ville parked on the roadside. Mickey is in the driver's seat with his feet on the dash watching Mallory dance on the hood of the car.

MICKEY
(*voiceover*)

And your dancing, my God, your dancing. I lie on my bed and go over every day, every minute of our happiness. Every day I take a day of our time and go through it hour by hour. I don't jump ahead either. I take it as it comes, and I live that day again. That way when I get to our first kiss . . .

DISSOLVE TO:

INT. A BEDROOM – NIGHT

The screen erupts with fire. Mickey and Mallory's faces appear in the flame kissing passionately.

                    MICKEY
                  (*voiceover*)
The killing of your parents, our wedding . . . They're not just
memories. I feel that joy again . . .

DISSOLVE TO:

INT. MALLORY'S CELL – DAY

*Not knowing where we are, camera moves across a wall into a CU of
Mallory.*

                    MICKEY
                  (*voiceover*)
Not the joy of taking a walk down memory lane, but because I do
the work I experience a chunk of the emotion I felt then. And I am
no longer in prison. There's no such thing as a prison. And when
my head hurts and I can remember no longer, I write you letters
and send them to your heart.

*When the letter is finished, Mallory gets off her bunk and goes to the
middle of the cell. She starts moving her body to music only she can hear,
then begins to sing the song 'Groove Me' in a slow a cappella, using the
cell as her stage and a man who isn't there as her audience.*

The song is completed in a single shot.

DISSOLVE TO:

INT. RESTAURANT – DAY

*Medium CU of Wayne holding a piece of paper in front of his face and
reading from it out loud. We hear Wayne's voice over Mallory's singing
before the last scene dissolves.*

                    WAYNE
                  (*reading out loud*)
'After taking a few days to reflect on your offer, I've come to the
conclusion that you are one hundred percent correct. A national
TV interview would be very advantageous to both Mallory and
me. The only obstacle is they're shipping me out to the funny
farm in four days. However, that is your problem and not mine.

                       24

I feel confident you'll manage. Here's to us making television history. Sincerely, Mickey Knox.'

Wayne drops the letter down from in front of his face.

Am I God or what?

We now see the restaurant adorned with the standard Denny's decor. Wayne's team is gathered in a booth that contains the remains of a greasy meal. In response to his last remark, they all pretend they are praying to him.

The team consists of Scott, the cameraman, who wears wild T-shirts (presently a T-shirt with the movie She Devils on Wheels *splashed on the front); Roger, the soundman, who wears wild Hawaiian shirts and Bermuda shorts; and Unruly Julie, Wayne's assistant, a young lady who wears Bermuda shorts, a baseball jersey, and a dark sports coat no matter how hot the weather is. Roger's never seen without his recorder, Scott's never without his camera, and Unruly Julie always has her giant notebook. These disheveled film types are all in their twenties and are a marked contrast to Wayne's stylish yuppie demeanor.*

Unruly Julie pops the cork on a champagne bottle. The guys hold out coffee mugs, which Julie fills. Julie, however, drinks straight from the bottle.

Note: This scene is to be played at a rapid fire 'His Girl Friday' pace.

WAYNE

Drink up! This is a celebration. This is the day we received word we were gonna make television history. We're gonna have the first sit-down, in-depth interview with the most charismatic serial killer ever, one day before he's being shipped to a mental hospital for the rest of his life. This is one of those golden moments that happens maybe only four times in a lucky journalist's career. This is Wallace with Noriega, this is Elton John confessing his bi-sexuality to the *Rolling Stone*, this is the tearful reporting of the Hindenberg disaster, this is Truffaut setting the record straight on Hitchcock, this is a Robert Capra photo, this is Woodward and Bernstein meeting Deep Throat in an underground parking lot, this is John Reed reporting 'The Ten Days That Shook the World,' this is the hippies' bloody palms at Kent State, the

Maysles brothers at Altamont, this is the Nixon/Frost
interviews . . .

ROGER

This is Raymond Burr witnessing the destruction of Tokyo by
Godzilla.

Everybody laughs.

SCOTT

What's the schedule, mein Führer?

*As Wayne talks, Unruly Julie writes furiously in her notebook. She never
speaks, just writes.*

WAYNE

We got tonight and tomorrow to get our shit together. The day
after that they're shippin' Mallory. That's when we do the Mickey
Knox interview 'cause the next day he goes.

SCOTT

Would the network really not run it without the interview?

WAYNE

Are you kidding? The last thing they expected was Mickey Knox
to get up close and personal. They wanted a follow-up episode and
would've taken anything I had given them. I'm not gonna tell
Mickey Knox that. I'm gonna make him think his grey matter
depends on it. When I told Woody and the brass about this coup,
they practically shit a brick. I'm talkin' an adobe brick. They want
to expand the show to a hour, and they want it on immediately.

ROGER

How immediate is immediately?

WAYNE

Next week's episode.

Wayne's team all spit out mouthfuls of champagne.

ROGER

We don't got enough footage for a hour follow-up.

WAYNE

Rape and pillage the first episode, just change the order a bit.

Those sons of bitches out there ain't gonna know the difference. All that shit is just filler for the interview anyway. We film a new intro. Show some old footage from the first episode so they get a brief history of Mickey and Mallory. We introduce a new angle – what the prison board is up to. We see some of that new shit, then the rest of the show is the interview. Now what's so fuckin' hard about that?

                    SCOTT
What camera do you want to use for the interview?

                    WAYNE
Fuck video. This is just too damned important. This is for posterity . . . No, we're using high contrast sixteen millimeter black and white, and I mean black and white, where the black's black and the white's white. Film . . . film . . . film!

CU of Unruly Julie writing in her notebook: 'Film . . . film . . . film!'

So Unruly Julie's comin' with me and planning the interview.
                (*points at Roger and Scott*)
You two go down to the editing bay, take the old footage and the new footage, put it together, and see what we got. Get it into shape so when we finish the interview, we can just stick it in.

                    SCOTT
When do you want the assembly?

                    WAYNE
Tomorrow.

CUT TO:

TITLE CARD: 'TOMORROW'

CUT TO:

INT. TV STATION – EDITING BAY – DAY

Camera follows behind Wayne, who's talking to Unruly Julie, who's writing furiously in her notebook.

WAYNE

At that point I'll ask him if he believes in God. If he says yes, I'll ask him what he thinks God would make of his actions. And is he worried about burning in hell? If he says no, I'll say, 'Well, Mickey, what *do* you believe in?' And hopefully, he'll say something like a live round of ammo, the expression on the face of a man he just split up the middle, Mallory's eyes, sex, drugs, and rock 'n' roll. He's bound to say something provocative.

Wayne and Unruly Julie enter the video editing room. Scott and Roger are sitting at the editing bay. Everybody is wearing, and looks like they slept in, the same clothes as the night before, except Wayne, who's in another sweater and looks alert and snappy.

OK, boys, let's have it.

SCOTT

Well, basically, what we did was put part of the old show on first . . .

ROGER

But we changed the order around so it wasn't super obvious . . .

SCOTT

Then we added the new shit to the tail . . .

ROGER

So we film the interview, and we can just slap it on at the end.

Wayne and Unruly Julie grab chairs and sit.

WAYNE

OK, let's see it.

CU of a video monitor screen. We see a show rewinding.

ROGER
(*off*)

Now we got to film a new intro for the follow-up episode. But we put the intro for the first episode at the beginning temporarily so you can see it with some scope.

WAYNE
(*voiceover*)

I hear ya. Play.

CU of Roger's hand pressing a play button.

The opening slate for 'American Maniacs' fills the screen.

TITLE CARD:

'MICKEY AND MALLORY'S REIGN OF TERROR'

EXT. HIGHWAY – DAY

Wayne Gayle is standing in the middle of an empty highway. The camera looks up from the ground.

With a wide angle lens, he looks practically mythic. Wayne speaks into the camera.

> WAYNE
> Hello. Welcome to 'American Maniacs.' I'm your host, Wayne Gayle. And this is Highway 58.

Wayne walks toward the camera. We dolly back.

> To some the fastest distance between point A and point B. To others a beautiful stretch of the American landscape. But to Mickey and Mallory Knox, it was a candy lane of murder and mayhem.

While we hear Wayne's narration, we see a montage of home 8mm movie footage. There are films of Mickey and Mallory living a normal life.

– Mickey shaking hands with the judge who married them. Mallory stands happily by Mickey's side.

– Mallory hamming up the sex angle, as she poses by Bob's Big Boy.

– Mallory sitting on Mickey's lap at home.

– CU on Mallory asleep in bed. Mickey (holding camera) tickles her under her chin. Mallory slaps herself in the face with a handful of shaving cream.

– Mickey and Mallory posing with Santa Clause.

-- Mickey being surprised on the toilet.

(*voiceover*)

After living a very routine, drab, nothing out-of-the-ordinary-ever-happens kind of life, the sweethearts shocked the entire nation with a cross-country crime and murder spree that lasted only three weeks, but left –

PHOTO: *black and white photos of bloody victims – men and women.*

PHOTO: *black and white photos of a bloodstained police chalk outline.*

(*voiceover*)
– forty-eight known bodies in its wake. Including –

8mm home movie footage of Mallory and her parents during happier times. All three are smiling. Mallory's in the middle with her arms around them. Mallory's father is eating a chicken drumstick. Mallory takes a bite out of it while he's holding it.

– Mallory's very own parents.

PHOTO: *color postcard of Los Angeles.*

They started their crimewave in Los Angeles.

Wayne Gayle stands in front of a Circle K convenience store. He speaks to us.

And they were finally apprehended here at this Circle K in St Paul, Minnesota.

CUT TO:

EXT. CIRCLE K – DAY

This sequence is filmed in 16mm color, cinéma-vérité *à la COPS.*

The camera runs behind three blue windbreaker-clad Cops, as they run up to the Circle K, shouting obscenities.

In front of the store three windbreaker Cops have Mickey on the ground, beating him with nightsticks. One Cop lies on the ground near them, holding his hands over his face, screaming.

To the left Mallory is slugging it out with a windbreaker Cop, matching him blow for blow.

Meanwhile, the three cops we ran with reach the action and join in.

MONTAGE:

– *Newspaper or magazine color ad for a 7-Eleven store.*

– *Newspaper or magazine color ad for a gas station.*

                    WAYNE
                  (*voiceover*)
They started off robbing 7-Eleven-type stores and gas stations and
later graduated to banks and the big time.

EXT. SUBURBAN STREET – DAY

*Wayne Gayle walks down the street. The camera walks with him. He
speaks into the camera.*

                    WAYNE
Mickey and Mallory's idea of an armed robbery was a little
different than most. It was an assault, actually.

INT. 7-ELEVEN STORE – DAY

*Wayne interviews Bishop, a young blond kid with a Flock of Seagulls
haircut. Bishop's name appears at the bottom of the screen.*

                    BISHOP
Well, I knew that Mickey and Mallory kill everybody when
they're through, except for one clerk. There were about four
people in the store then, and I was working with Stevo. And I like
Stevo, you know? But I was thinking, what could I do to make
them pick me to be the clerk that gets to live?

INT. 7-ELEVEN STORE – DAY

*This scene is shot through the store's black and white video surveillance
camera. The date and time of day are burned into edges of the frame.*

*Mickey and Mallory charge into a 7-Eleven store, cocking their shotguns
and shouting things.*

Mickey shoots a customer who lies on the ground screaming.

31

Mallory blasts a female customer, holding a Big Gulp. She flies into the comic book rack.

Mickey points his shotgun at Bishop the store clerk and screams:

>MICKEY
>
>Money! Money! Money! Fast! Fast! Faster! Faster! Faster than that!

Bishop stuffs money in a bag as Mallory guards the door, shotgun ready.

Stevo, the other store clerk, walks in from the back room carrying boxes and wearing a Walkman.

Mickey and Mallory spin round and shoot him.

All this mayhem happens before our disbelieving eyes with Wayne's narration over it.

>WAYNE
>(*voiceover*)
>
>They'd storm in with shotguns, and kill every customer in the place right off the bat.

CUT TO:

Smiling photos of other victims. We cut from each photo to the next photo after shotgun fire.

EXT. BLEACHERS – DAY

Wayne Gayle sitting on football bleachers. He stares into the camera for a few beats. Then, after his dramatic silence, he talks.

>WAYNE
>
>Sick, isn't it?
>(*mournful pause*)
>
>After killing numerous people, they would always leave one clerk alive. One clerk . . . to give them the money, and tell the tale of –

PHOTO: *black and white snapshot of Mickey and Mallory standing next to each other, guns in hand, smiling for the camera.*
>(*voiceover*)
>
>Mickey and Mallory.

PHOTO: *Police Academy black and white snapshot of Officer Gerald Nash.*

Patrolman Gerald Nash was just one of the twelve peace officers that Mickey and Mallory murdered during their reign of terror.

PHOTO: *black and white photo of Gerald Nash and his partner Dale Wrigley, dressed in their uniforms, arms around each other.*

Gerald and his partner Dale Wrigley were parked at . . .

PHOTO: *black and white snapshot of donut shop.*

. . . this donut shop, Alfie's Donuts. When –

Interview with Dale Wrigley. Dale's name appears below him on the screen.

> DALE
> This '68 Cadillac Coupe de Ville pulled up about three spaces away. Gerald came walking out with our coffee and –
> *(begins to tear up)*
> my bear claw. When the driver of the car asked him something, Gerald started giving him what looked like street directions. When he finished, the driver waved him 'thanks,' brought up a shotgun and –

PHOTO: *black and white of donut shop.*

WIDER PHOTO: *Alfie's Donuts and parking lot. On this photo, a white grease pencil circles where Gerald was shot. We hear a shotgun blast and a scream over this.*

PHOTO: *black and white of Mickey and Mallory. We hear laughter and a car peeling out over this.*

EXT. BLEACHERS – DAY

Wayne talks to us.

> WAYNE
> Apparently bored with banditry and murder, the two outlaws proved what renaissance psychopaths they really are. To break up the monotony in between bank jobs, or what have you, they started butchering whole households at random.

CUT TO:

Montage of newspaper front-page stories and headlines of family households butchered by the Knoxes.

INT. WAYNE'S STUDIO – DAY

Wayne, dressed in a pink shirt and suspenders, talks to us in front of a blue screen that has 'Wayne Gayle's American Maniacs' logo behind him.

> WAYNE
>
> Unfortunately, the story didn't end with their capture. It just became more surreal. Their subsequent trial turned into a sick circus . . .

CUT TO:

EXT. COURTHOUSE – DAY

The camera captures the crowd in front of the courthouse. They're a very mixed lot.

> WAYNE
> (*voiceover*)
>
> . . . As spectators, reporters, law students, tourists, gawkers, the interested, the curious, the devoted, and the demented were drawn to the Los Angeles county courthouse like moths to a flame.

INT. WAYNE'S STUDIO – DAY

Wayne talks to us.

> WAYNE
>
> The Mickey and Mallory Knox murder trial was so event-filled it made the crime spree that took place before pale in comparison. The first point was the decision of Mickey's to act as his own counsel. Now this in itself is not unheard of, for instance, Ted Bundy acted as his own counsel as well. What was unexpected was how good Mickey's performance would be.

34

INT. JUDGE'S DEN – DAY

Interview with Judge Burt Steinsma in his den at home.

> WAYNE
> (*voiceover*)
> We spoke with Burt Steinsma, who was the presiding judge
> during the Knox trial.

> JUDGE STEINSMA
> Mickey was surprisingly effective. When I was told I was to be the
> judge of this trial and then I was told Mickey Knox would be
> handling his own defense, I got a headache that lasted five days.
> But soon I breathed a sigh of relief. Mickey showed up very
> prepared, and proved to be an excellent amateur lawyer.

INT. WANDA BISBING'S OFFICE – DAY

*Interview with state prosecutor Wanda Bisbing, an attractive woman in
her forties.*

> WAYNE
> (*voiceover*)
> However, this opinion isn't shared by the state's prosecutor on
> this case, Wanda Bisbing.

Wayne's with Bisbing.

Judge Steinsma said that Mickey showed up very prepared and
proved to be an excellent amateur attorney.

> BISBING
> Oh, that's rich. Well, considering that Mickey Knox turned his
> court into a mockery and personally made him look like a fool, I'd
> say that's very benevolent of Judge Steinsma. As far as Mickey
> being an excellent amateur lawyer, maybe I'm old-fashioned, but
> when I went to law school, we were taught the object was to win
> the case, which I did.

INT. WAYNE'S STUDIO – DAY

Wayne talks to us.

The nation caught fire to Mickey and Mallory fever, Mickey and Mallory mania, if you will, as the merits to Mickey's talent as a defense attorney became apparent.

Law students from all ends of the country converged on Los Angeles as legal history took a new course. But that was only the lemon next to the pie. And that pie is you, the American people. That pie is the way the strangely charismatic – and make no mistake, they are charismatic – Mickey and Mallory have captured the public's interest, fear, and, in some cases, admiration.

CUT TO:

EXT. COURTHOUSE STEPS – DAY

Wayne interviews three long-haired guys: Chuck, Steve, and Jeff.

WAYNE
What do you think of Mickey and Mallory?

CHUCK
Hot.

JEFF
Hot.

STEVE
Totally hot.

CHUCK
Mickey and Mallory's the best thing to happen to mass murder since Manson.

STEVE
Forty-eight people known. They're way cooler than Manson.

Wayne interviews Morgan and Page, two young girls.

WAYNE
What do you think of Mickey and Mallory?

MORGAN
Well, he's just . . . I dunno . . . charismatic.

They're so romantic.

Wayne interviews an intense Cop.

                    INTENSE COP
I'm here to watch the judge give those two shit asses (bleep) the
stiffest sentence the law allows. I want to see their faces when the
state says they are the worst scum-sucking, degenerate, douche-
bag, filthy, I don't know whats ever shit (bleep) out.
                (referring to crowd behind him)
And these assholes (bleep) are making heroes outta sickos. You
wanna know who a hero is? You wanna know? I'll tell ya who a
goddamn hero is. Mike Griffin. Mike fuckin' (bleep) Griffin is
who these misguided assholes (bleep) should be revering. You
know why Mike Jerome Griffin is a hero? I'll tell ya why. Because
he was killed in the line of duty. Do you want to know how he
died?

                    WAYNE
Yes.

                    INTENSE COP
I'll tell you. Mike Jerome Griffin was killed in the line of duty by
those two anti-heroes.

Wayne interviews Russell Vossler, Harvard law student.

                    WAYNE
Tell me, Mr Vossler, how many days of the trial have you
attended?

                    RUSSELL
Ahhh yesss, I've been fortunate enough to attend two days. Law
history in the making. I've been a participant.

                    WAYNE
And you being a Harvard law student, what is your opinion of
Mickey Knox's performance.

                    RUSSELL
Ahhh, Mickey's pistolero savvy in the courtroom trial rivals, dare
I say, conquers that of master Melvin Belli. He's like a

magnificent loose cannon, firing point-blank range in the prosecutor's face. It is my anticipation –

BACK TO: THE LONG-HAIRED GUYS

> WAYNE
> You're talking about a man and a woman who killed innocent people.

> STEVE
> Don't get us wrong . . .

> CHUCK
> We respect human life and all.

> JEFF
> It's a tragedy.

> STEVE
> But . . . if I was a serial killer, which I'm not, but if I was, I'd be like Mickey.

Wayne's talking with Marvin, a black man.

> MARVIN
> They're like that crazy mother in the first Dirty Harry movie. Member that crazy ass mother? They're like him. Mickey and Mallory be doin' some cold-blooded shit. When I hear about some of the shit they be doin' on TV, I say, 'Damn, that's fucked (bleep) up.'

BACK TO: THE TWO YOUNG GIRLS.

> PAGE
> (*laughing and blushing*)
> We sit in the courtroom all day and try to catch Mickey's eye.

CUT TO:

INT. GOLD'S GYM – DAY

Wayne's sitting in the gym. Behind him Muscle Men are working out. Their grunting sounds fill the background.

Wayne looks up and just off camera to the people he's interviewing.

                    WAYNE
What do you think of Mickey and Mallory?

*Extreme CU on Simon and Norman Hun, two brothers/bodybuilders, in
a head shot.*

                    SIMON
I admire them.

                    NORMAN
I do, too.

                    WAYNE
                   (*confused*)
But how can you say that?

                    SIMON
They're mesmerizing.

                    NORMAN
Hypnotizing.

                    SIMON
Have you seen *Pumping Iron*?

                    WAYNE
Yes.

                    NORMAN
Then you've seen the scene where Arnold Schwartzenegger is
talking to Lou Ferigno.

                    WAYNE
Yes.

                    SIMON
Through the power of the simple word –

                    NORMAN
And a snake-eye glare.

                    SIMON
– and a snake-eye glare, Arnold was able to totally psyche out any
confidence Ferigno had.

NORMAN

He squashed him mentally before physically defeating him.

SIMON

He had the edge. The mind's edge.

NORMAN

Mickey and Mallory have that edge.

SIMON

Only on a much grander scale.

NORMAN

They've hypnotized the nation.

SIMON

Schwartzenegger was the king of the edge before they came along.

The CU of the brothers zooms back.

WAYNE

You say this and yet . . . you two are both victims of Mickey and Mallory.

Shot has zoomed back to reveal that both Simon and Norman are in wheelchairs (their legs maimed or gone).

SIMON

Yes.

NORMAN

Yes.

WAYNE

How can you say that you 'admire' them?

NORMAN

It's like this, Wayne. Two people are standing in a dark room waiting for the other to attack. These two people can't see each other, yet they know they're there. Now, they can either stand in that dark room forever, waiting until they die of boredom, or one of them can make the first move.

WAYNE

Why can't they just shake hands and be friends?

NORMAN

They can't because neither knows if the other is a deranged senseless killer like the Knoxes. So, you may as well make the first move.

WAYNE

And they made the first move?

NORMAN

Unfortunately, yes.

SIMON

But you see, that's OK, Wayne.

WAYNE

Why?

SIMON

They passed the 'edge' along to us.

WAYNE

How so?

SIMON

By taking away our legs. Now we have to fight harder to get ahead than anyone else you'll find in this gym. Probably the whole city. They gave us the fighting spirit. Before this happened I was content. Now I'm pissed off. Now I'm half a man and I've got to work like the devil to get whole again.

WAYNE

But you'll never be whole again.

SIMON

Never is a very long time, Wayne. A word only the weak use. I'm not a sore loser. Even if I don't have a leg to stand on, I'm going to get up and fight this world until I'm on top again.

NORMAN

That's the Mickey and Mallory way.

SIMON

And that's the way of the world.

NORMAN

They're just shocking the world into remembering the primal law.

SIMON

Survival of the fittest.

WAYNE

One last question. Usually Mickey and Mallory kill all of their victims. Why did they let you two survive?

The brothers pause, then turn to Wayne.

NORMAN

They had us tied down during one of their house raids, you've seen the headlines, and they were taking a chainsaw to our legs before they were gonna kill us.

SIMON

Just for fun, I guess.

NORMAN

And then Mallory stops Mickey and says, 'Hey, these are the Brothers Hun.'

SIMON

Mickey stops sawin' on my leg and says, 'Oh my God, I'm your biggest fan!'

NORMAN

Apparently, they've seen all our films.

SIMON

They were especially influenced by *Conquering Huns of Neptune*.

NORMAN

So, Mallory calls 911 and they took off.

SIMON

They actually apologized.

INT. WAYNE'S STUDIO – DAY

WAYNE

The couple proved so popular that a motion picture glamorizing their exploits was made . . .

CUT TO:

A poster for the Mickey and Mallory movie Thrill Killers. *It has a drawing of the Movie Mickey and Movie Mallory in a romantic pose à la* Gone With the Wind, *both with guns in their hands. Around them are smaller drawings of cars, people shooting, people fighting, explosions, etc.*

The ad-lines are: 'RIPPED FROM TODAY'S HEADLINES – THE TRUE STORY OF MICKEY AND MALLORY.' 'THE COUPLE THAT LIVED FOR LOVE AND LOVED TO KILL.'

The poster lists the credits: 'Starring Jessie Alexander Warwick and Buffy St McQueen.' 'Written and Directed by Neil Pope.'

WAYNE
(*voiceover*)

The movie *Thrill Killers* proved to be a tremendous box-office success, making stars out of the before then unknown –

CUT TO:

Stills of Movie Mickey and Movie Mallory holding weapons, posing together, creating mayhem.

– actors Jessie Alexander Warwick and Buffy St McQueen.

CUT TO:

Movie trailer for Thrill Killers:

Shot of Movie Mickey dressed in a fast-food uniform.

ANNOUNCER
(*voiceover*)

Meet Mickey Knox!

MOVIE MICKEY

I'm gettin' off this minimum wage train. Break my back for you and throw away my youth for nothing. When I'm thirty, have a big wall drop down in front of me called the future. Realize I've been doin' time in a burger flippin' jail.

He rips off his uniform.

Listen to me, Jimmy-dick, I want cash, lots of it, cars, fast cars! And I want it now! Not later, now! I wanna wail, baby, wail!

Shot of Movie Mallory on her hands and knees crawling toward camera.

43

ANNOUNCER
(*voiceover*)

And his lovely wife Mallory.

MOVIE MALLORY

I need ya, Mickey. I gotta have ya. I'm no good for no one else. When I'm with you, I burn, baby. Burn like blue flame.

Shot of Movie Mickey and Movie Mallory driving fast and laughing their heads off.

ANNOUNCER
(*voiceover*)

Together they're the Thrill Killers. The true story of the couple that shocked the world . . .

Shot of the Movie Knoxes firing guns.

. . . with a bloodlust of violence . . .

Shot of Movie Mickey and Movie Mallory kissing.

. . . and unbridled passion.

Shot of Movie Mallory with a knife to a Cop's throat. Movie Mickey holds a shotgun.

MOVIE COP

When society catches up with you, I'd hate to be in your boots.

MOVIE MICKEY

Let me tell ya about society and its boots. It uses those boots for steppin' on people like me and her!

CUT TO:

INT. EDITING ROOM – DAY

Wayne enters an editing room where film-maker Neil Pope is working at a Moviola.

WAYNE
(*voiceover*)

We talked with Neil Pope, writer and director of *Thrill Killers*, for his take on the Mickey and Mallory phenomenon.

Pope stops the movieola, turns toward the camera, and greets Wayne MOS.

CUT INTO INTERVIEW:

NEIL POPE

It is my belief that Mickey and Mallory Knox are a cultural phenomenon that could only exist in our sexually repressed society. A flower that could only bloom amidst a grotesque fast-food culture. And what I tried to do with *Thrill Killers* was trace the root of the problem all the way down the vine to the original bad seed. Yet amidst the violence and murder and carnage, you've got the structure of a Wagnerian love story.

EXT. ALLEY – DAY

In a back alley, the conclusion of Thrill Killers *plays out. The sounds of sirens and choppers are nearing. Movie Mickey, shotgun in hand, runs down the alley, stopping at a dumpster, where the wounded and bloody Movie Mallory sits propped up against a brick wall. On the bottom of the screen, the subtitle appears: Scene from* Thrill Killers (*1990*).

MOVIE MALLORY

Mickey, honey, listen to me.

Movie Mallory holds out her hand for him to take. He does.

I can't go. I'm too fucked up.

MOVIE MICKEY

I'm not saying it's not gonna hurt, but –

MOVIE MALLORY

I can't run with you, Mickey! I really want to. If I could, I would, but I can't. I gotta stay here. But you can still get out of here.

MOVIE MICKEY

No fuckin' way! No fuckin' way!

MOVIE MALLORY

If you stay, they'll catch you, and they don't have to catch you –

MOVIE MICKEY

No fuckin' way!

MOVIE MALLORY

Mickey, you're wasting time!

MOVIE MICKEY

I don't give a damn if a million United States marines, all whistling
'The Halls of Montezuma', are gonna come marchin' down this
alley any second. There ain't no fuckin' way in hell I'm leaving you.
And that's that!

Movie Mallory grabs his hand with both of hers. She's crying.

The siren and chopper sounds are getting closer.

MOVIE MALLORY

Mickey, my love, if you leave me, they'll catch me and take me to
the hospital. If you stay, you'll make 'em kill you. Then it'd be like I
killed you. I could bear anything, but I couldn't bear that. So
please, please, please, please, for me, my handsome husband, run
for your life.

The sirens and choppers draw nearer.

MOVIE MICKEY

I can't do it. You're my wife, you're my partner. A fella doesn't run
when his partner can't run with him. Mallory, my angel, if I could
of left ya, I'd of left ya a long time ago.

They kiss.

MOVIE MALLORY

Well, hell, if you won't leave, give me a gun so I can go out shooting.

Movie Mickey hands her his .44 Magnum from his belt.

MOVIE MICKEY

Sit tight. I'm gonna make it a little tougher for 'em.

*Movie Mickey runs to the end of the alley, peers around the corner at the
arriving Cops.*

(*to himself*)

Time to get naked and boogie.

*Movie Mallory is out of Movie Mickey's view. She cocks the .44, then
places the barrel under her chin.*

46

MOVIE MALLORY

Mickey!

Movie Mickey's busy. He doesn't turn around.

MOVIE MICKEY

Yes.

MOVIE MALLORY

You made every day like kindergarten.

Movie Mallory pulls the trigger. Bang!

Dolly down the alley to a CU on Movie Mickey as he spins around.

Movie Mallory literally blows her head clean off. Her headless body, gun in hand, remains upright in her sitting position.

Movie Mickey runs toward her, screaming her name in slow motion.

MOVIE MICKEY

Mallory!

CUT TO: THE POPE INTERVIEW

WAYNE
(*off*)

Why did you kill Mallory? Both of them are still alive.

NEIL POPE

It was dramatic license, no doubt. But I felt an operatic love story needed an operatic ending. The two of them kill for each other. They offer the death of their victims to each other like other lovers offer flowers or bonbons. So what more natural, what more organic, what more poetic than Mallory offering her death to Mickey? It's where it's been leading since day one. We worked it in the movie by using a 'what if they escaped' situation. I think it works beautifully. You'd be surprised. People come up to me at the end of the movie in tears.

EXT. PARKING LOT — DAY

Actor Jessie Alexander Warwick sits on his motorcycle and talks to the camera. He's dressed in a Levi's jacket, jeans, a bandana is wrapped around his head, and as he talks he bogarts a smoke. His name appears at the bottom of the screen.

                              JESSIE
One thing about Mickey for sure, he's definitely a man who has his moments. It was wild playin' him. It was one of those get-it-out-of-your-system performances.

INT. BUFFY ST MCQUEEN'S HOME – DAY

This interview is shot in Buffy's house à la Barbara Walters. Buffy sits on the couch in her living room with a cat in her lap. From time to time, she sips from a coffee cup. Her name appears at the bottom of the screen.

                              BUFFY
I didn't play Mallory the murderer. I didn't play her as a butcher. I played her as a woman in love, who also happens to murder people. I didn't want her to be at arm's length from the audience or myself. If you play her as this wild maniac, the audience never has to deal with her. If you see a decapitation in a movie, you just say 'Oh wow, a neat special effect.' Because you can't relate to a decapitation. It doesn't mean anything to anybody because it's not personal. Decapitations don't fall into most people's realm of life experiences. But if you show somebody in a movie getting a paper cut, the whole audience squirms. Because everybody can relate to a paper cut.

                              WAYNE
                              (off)
Did you meet the real Mallory Knox?

                              BUFFY
I tried to, but she wouldn't see me. But I read some letters she wrote to Mickey before the murder spree. They helped me out a lot.

EXT. PARKING LOT – DAY

Jessie talks to camera.

48

WAYNE
(*off*)
You met Mickey Knox, didn't you?

JESSIE
Yeah, I visited him when he was up in Susanville. He's a little
cerebral for my taste, but all in all, we got along.

INT. OFFICE – DAY

*Wayne, sitting in a chair in front of a desk, interviews Dr Reinghold,
who sits behind the desk.*

WAYNE
(*voiceover*)
To get a psychiatric view on the strange attraction Mickey and
Mallory seem to have, we talked with Dr Emil Reinghold, noted
psychologist and author.

Wayne begins his interview.

Can you shed some light, Dr Reinghold, on why the public has
taken a pair of sociopaths so close to their bosom?

DR REINGHOLD
Well, for one, the media has done a tremendous job of turning the
husband and wife mass murderers into celebrities. But it's the
country's youth who have turned the couple into the ultimate
anti-heroes. Basically, the very thing that makes them most lethal
is the exact same thing that captures the public's hearts and minds
– Mickey and Mallory's operatic devotion to each other. In a
world where people can't seem to make the simplest of
relationships work and the slightest emotional commitment is
considered devastating, Mickey and Mallory have a do-or-die
romance of a Shakespearian magnitude. To the country's youth,
seventy-five percent of whom are coming from broken homes,
that's appealing. They have an 'us against the world' posture
which always appeals to the youth. And they've taken that posture
seventeen steps beyond.
   It's not 'us against the world,' it's 'we're gonna kill the world.'
They're exciting. I read their file and I find myself turning the

49

pages like it was a paperback. Why do disillusioned youths get
into Mickey and Mallory? Why do disillusioned housewives read
romance novels? Why are you filming this special? Because you
know as well as I do, you say 'tonight at nine Charles Manson
speaks,' everybody's going to tune in to hear what he says. Mickey
and Mallory have shocked a country numb with violence. They've
created a world where only two exist and anybody who
inadvertently enters that world is murdered.

EXT. COURTHOUSE – DAY

Shots of the crowd.

> WAYNE
> (*voiceover*)
> This attitude from the young toward their ultimate anti-heroes is
> nationwide. And spreading.

Two London Teens, Boy and Girl, dressed like the Knoxes.

TITLE CARD:

'LONDON'

> LONDON BOY
> You take all the great figures from the states . . . Elvis, Jack
> Kerouac, Bukowski, James Dean, Jim Morrison, Angela Davis,
> Jack Nicholson, Jim Thompson, Martin Scorsese . . . add a
> fuckin' (bleep) pile of nitro and you got Mickey and Mallory.
> They're like rebels without a cause, except they have a cause.
> Only nobody knows what it is.

> LONDON GIRL
> (*screaming*)
> Their cause is each uvver!

*Two Japanese Teens, Boy and Girl, dressed like the Knoxes. They speak
in Japanese, which is translated into English.*

TITLE CARD:

'JAPAN'

As Japanese Boy and Girl speak, we hear:

TRANSLATOR
(*voiceover*)
Keep the faith, Mickey and Mallory, keep the faith.

Two French Teens, Boy and Girl, dressed like the Knoxes. They speak in French, and we hear the translation in English.

TITLE CARD:
'FRANCE'

TRANSLATOR
(*voiceover*)
Mickey and Mallory have a love that's L.A.M.F.

FRENCH BOY
(*in English*)
They are super cool!

INT. WAYNE'S STUDIO – DAY

WAYNE
And as to almost give this whole misplaced admiration scenario a cherry on the top, the rock band Redd Kross entered the charts last week at number 13 with their song 'Natural Born Killers: The Saga of Mickey and Mallory.'

CUT TO:

A clip from the Redd Kross video of 'Natural Born Killers.'

BACK TO: WAYNE'S STUDIO

WAYNE
The third wicked twist to this story is Grace Mulberry.

CUT TO:

Front page newspaper.

Headline reads: 'MICKEY AND MALLORY KILL SIX TEENS DURING SLUMBER PARTY!' *In smaller bold face under it:* 'One Teen Escapes Killers' Clutches.' *On the front page is a photo of the teen who escaped. It's seventeen-year-old Grace Mulberry. Camera moves into CU of the photo.*

                         WAYNE
                       (*voiceover*)
Of the six teens murdered that night, seventeen-year-old Grace
Mulberry was the lucky one left to tell the tale. And this haunted
young lady summoned up the courage to take the stand, tell what
she saw that horrible night, and then allow herself to be cross-
examined by the man who killed her brother and girlfriends.

EXT. COURTHOUSE — DAY

All kinds of people are gathered around. It's a real media event.

*Grace's sedan pulls up to the courthouse. The many spectators and
reporters surround the car.*

*Grace, her Father, and Bisbing emerge from the sedan, and start walking
up the courthouse steps.*

Microphones and cameras are thrust at her as Reporters ask questions.

*Grace is afraid to face the crowd. Her head darts in the direction of each
question, but she doesn't answer. She remains silent and scared.*

               FEMALE ORIENTAL REPORTER
Miss Mulberry! How does it feel to be the only survivor of Mickey
and Mallory's reign of terror?

                   FAT MALE REPORTER
Miss Mulberry! Has the experience marked you?

Some scruffy Transient sticks his head in Grace's face.

                       TRANSIENT
Did ya watch your brother get stabbed up?

                         WAYNE
How do you feel about Mickey cross-examining you?

*Grace, her Father, and Bisbing shove their way through the crowd. After
Grace and her entourage enter the courthouse, we hear the cry of:*

                         VOICE
                         (*off*)
Mickey and Mallory!

                          52

Camera whips toward the bottom of the steps as the car carrying Mickey and Mallory pulls up. The Reporters race down the steps they just raced up. The Mickey and Mallory fans go apeshit.

Mickey and Mallory, handcuffed, are being led up the steps by Sheriff's Deputies. Wayne Gayle and other Reporters film them and shoot out questions. Microphones are thrust into their faces.

WAYNE

Mickey, how do you feel about cross-examining Grace Mulberry?

MICKEY

I'm keen with anticipation.

FEMALE ORIENTAL REPORTER

What do you think of this turn-out, Mallory?

MALLORY

I ain't never had so much fun.

A Cute Reporter, a Tawny Little type, steps forward.

CUTE REPORTER

Do you have any regrets?

MALLORY

Not a one.

MICKEY

Yeah, I always regretted we never got around to looking up my old history teacher, Miss Bainbridge. Now there's a big bad bitch not good for herself or nobody.

BLACK REPORTER

What's your favorite pastime?

MICKEY

You mean aside from what I'm being tried for?

Mallory playfully elbows Mickey in his ribs.

Oh, I'd say watching TV.

All the Reporters in unison:

                    REPORTERS
What's your favorite show?

                    MICKEY
Have Gun Will Travel.

                    CUTE REPORTER
Do you have anything to say to your fans?

                    MICKEY
                (looking into camera)
You ain't seen nothin' yet.

CUT TO:

EXT. COURTHOUSE – DAY

Wayne by himself standing on the courthouse steps.

                    WAYNE
                (to camera)
No, apparently we had not seen everything. Grace Mulberry gave
her tearful testimony. Then it was Mickey Knox's turn for cross-
examination.

CUT TO:

COURT SKETCH: *An artist's sketch of Mickey cross-examining Grace on
the stand.*

                    BISBING
                (voiceover)
Grace was terrified of Mickey. You have to understand most of
their victims were normal people with normal lives that nothing
out of the ordinary ever happens to.

COURT SKETCH: *Mickey looking like the devil himself.*

Then out of the blue, they're dealing with the devil incarnate. It
was extremely difficult for us to find survivors who would take the
stand and testify when they knew Mickey would be cross-
examining them.

COURT SKETCH: *Grace, terrified.*

Grace was every bit as terrified, every bit as haunted.

CUT TO:

Wanda Bisbing, the DA. Her name appears at the bottom of the screen.

But she felt her brother Tim and her five girlfriends were counting on her.

CUT TO:

INT. WAYNE'S STUDIO – DAY

Wayne walks into a CU.

> WAYNE
> What you are now about to see is the courtroom video footage shot by the state as part of its records. We would like to warn you at this time that, if you have children watching this show, they should leave the room at this point.

CUT TO:

INT. COURTROOM – DAY

Note: The following is to be covered from one camera position from the back of the courtroom and will follow the action in medium to extreme CUs.

Note: The dialogue will be very distant and hollow (sometimes inaudible). The sequence will employ the use of sub-titles.

Bisbing is wrapping up her examination of Grace, who sits at the witness stand. Judge Steinsma sits at his bench.

> BISBING
> (off)
> No further questions, Your Honor.

An emotional pause as we concentrate on Grace. Silence.

> JUDGE STEINSMA
> (off)
> Would you care to cross-examine the witness, Mr Knox?

MICKEY

As a matter of fact, Your Honor, I would.

Mickey enters the frame, pacing back and forth with a pencil pressed to his lips in thought.

Grace pulls out a reserve of strength. Her eyes come up and lock, hatefully, on Mickey.

MICKEY

That's one helluva story, Miss Mulberry.

GRACE

Yes. It is.

MICKEY

Grace . . . I hope you don't mind if I call you Grace . . . I'd like to talk to you about your late brother, Tim, if you feel up to it.

Mickey leaves the frame. We hold on CU of Grace.

(*off*)

Did you get along?

Grace doesn't answer.

Miss Mulberry?

GRACE

More or less.

MICKEY
(*off*)

What do you mean by that?

GRACE

Well, he's my older brother. When we were growing up, there were times we could very well of done without each other. But when it counted, we were close.

Mickey re-enters frame.

MICKEY

I'd like to talk about Tim's martial arts abilities. How long had he been studying?

56

GRACE

He started when he was in the seventh grade, so that would make it nine years.

MICKEY

When you study the martial arts, they give out belts that come in different colors to signify what level you're at in your training. Am I correct on that point?

GRACE

Yes, you are.

MICKEY

What was the color of Tim's belt?

GRACE

The style of fighting that Tim studied didn't believe in belts.

MICKEY

Is that a fact? Well then, Grace, could you tell us what form of martial arts it was that Tim was schooled in?

GRACE

Tim studied several styles, but his favorite was Jeet Kune Do.

MICKEY

Jeet Kune Do . . . Now I did some research on that form of fighting, and I found out that Jeet Kune Do was a style developed by Bruce Lee. Did you know that?

GRACE

Yes, I did. That's why Tim studied it. Because it was Bruce Lee's fighting style.

MICKEY

Now, while I freely admit total ignorance on the subject, I have heard of Bruce Lee. And I was under the impression that Bruce Lee was one of, if not *the* greatest fighter in the history of martial arts.

GRACE

That's what Tim said.

MICKEY

So, I think it would be safe to say that anybody who studied for nine years the fighting style that Bruce Lee, arguably the greatest martial artist of all time, developed, that would be a fella who could defend himself. Would you describe Tim that way, Grace?

GRACE

Yes, I would.

Mickey points at Grace with the pencil in his hand.

MICKEY

Point of fact, weren't Tim's hands registered as lethal weapons?

GRACE

Yes, they were.

MICKEY

That means his hands are considered a weapon like a gun or a knife. Am I correct on that point?

GRACE

Yes, you are.

MICKEY

Yet, in your testimony just now, you described how Tim kicked me four times in the head.

Mickey again walks from the frame and we concentrate on Grace.

(*off*)

And his trained martial artist's kicks had little to no effect . . .

Grace looks down to her folded hands.

Then, after shrugging off four blows to the head like I was Superman, I lifted Tim-nine-years-of-Jeet-Kune-Do-Mulberry off the ground and threw him across the room.

Grace looks up as Mickey enters frame with the knife from the evidence table raised over his head.

Then I took this knife and proceeded to tear him limb from limb. And this man, whose hands are lethal weapons –

58

BISBING

Objection, defense is intimidating the witness with the murder weapon.

JUDGE STEINSMA

Mr Knox! Put that knife down!

MICKEY

– had little to no defense.

GRACE
(*yelling*)

I don't know how you did it, but you did it!

Mickey lowers the knife.

MICKEY

How do you think a human being could possibly be capable of doing something like that?

GRACE
(*yelling*)

I don't know!

MICKEY

Now . . . I don't believe that, Grace. I think you have a definite opinion on how I was able to do those things you described. Now, I'm going to ask you again. And I want you to remember you are under oath.

Grace collects herself.

In your opinion, Miss Mulberry, how was I able to murder your brother Tim Mulberry in the manner you described?

GRACE
(*softly*)

You're not human.

Mickey raises his arms in a show of victory and turns to the court and the jury.

I thought about it a lot. And the only thing I could figure is that you're not human.

Mickey laughs. Grace clutches her temples to stop her pain.

You're a vampire, or the devil, or a monster, or a cyborg, or something like that. But you're not human.

MICKEY

Thank you. Thank you, Grace. There is but one other thing I would like you to share with this court.

Grace tearfully looks up and meets Mickey's demonic glare as he turns to her.

GRACE

Yes . . .

In a flash Mickey charges the witness stand and plunges the knife deep into Grace's chest. General pandemonium breaks loose in the courtroom as Mickey's vicious attack continues. Camera goes haywire; zooming in to capture Grace's death in CU.

Screams of pain and horror fill the court. Our view is blocked temporarily but is regained in time to see a blood-soaked and triumphant Mickey turn from Grace's lifeless body.

Freeze frame on Mickey.

DISSOLVE TO:

EXT. COURTHOUSE REAR – DAY

Mickey, dressed in county blues, is led out of the courtroom by Sheriff's Deputies. He's cuffed hand and leg. Reporters throw out questions, photographers shoot photos; Mickey is somewhere else, no mugging to the crowd this time.

WAYNE
(voiceover)

After the deadly brouhaha in the courtroom, the judge, honorable Burt Steinsma, passed down a sentence that was to make legal history.

INT. JUDGE'S DEN – DAY

Interview with Judge Steinsma in his den at home.

MOS shot of Wayne and Judge talking.

> WAYNE
> (*voiceover*)
> We spoke with retired Judge Steinsma at his home in Baltimore,
> Maryland.

The interview:

> WAYNE
> Was there any vengeance on your part with your unique sentence?

> JUDGE STEINSMA
> Yes, unquestionably. After they did what they did in my court,
> any judge worth his robe will tell you the same thing. It couldn't
> help but affect my decision. That's why they have judges. We're
> supposed to be fair to a fault, but when it's showtime, we have to
> make a decision. That's why we don't just input all the facts into a
> computer for the appropriate punishment. I couldn't give them
> the death penalty. See, California hops back and forth on that
> subject. Mickey and Mallory went to court when it was out of
> favor, which is actually good because it leaves more room for
> imagination. Anybody can give somebody the chair. When you
> have someone who deserves to die and you can't kill them, you
> have to be creative. And if the bastards had let it stand, it would
> have been the perfect sentence. It hit 'em right where they lived.
> Far more punishing than the death penalty.

> WAYNE
> Would you please describe for our audience what your sentence
> was?

> JUDGE STEINSMA
> Well, in a rogue's gallery of killers, Mickey and Mallory are very
> unique. I've seen a lot of killers in my day, and they're a very cold
> lot. They have no more feelings about taking a person's life than
> squashing a tiny bug. It's all the same to them.
> Well, Mickey and Mallory were that 'kill 'em to watch their
> expression change' attitude personified. Except with each other.

61

And, since they lived only for each other, I wanted to attack that, at its very root. So, in a nutshell, my sentence was double life for each without any possibility for parole. That would be fairly standard in their case. The twist I added was that husband and wife would have no contact or correspondence with each other for the rest of their lives. And they would never receive any word or information about the other. So basically, once the cell door slams shut, Mickey and Mallory will completely disappear from each other's life. They'll never even know when the other dies. But alas, the best laid plans of mice and men . . .

CUT TO:

EXT. COURTHOUSE REAR – DAY

Mallory in tears, hysterical, is cuffed hand to foot, and being dragged by Sheriff's Deputies into the prison bus. Reporters throw out questions, photographers shoot photos, TV news people capture the moment on video.

The bus pulls out on to the street.

CUT TO:

PHOTO: *Mickey in prison uniform being led by guards.*

PHOTO: *Shot through bars of Mallory in her cell. Her back is to the camera.*

WAYNE
(*voiceover*)

The sentence was never to reach that point. Because after only a year, Mickey and Mallory created so much mayhem that it was decided . . .

INSERT: *Front page newspaper:* 'MICKEY AND MALLORY TO BE TRANSFERRED TO ASYLUM.'

. . . that they were mentally ill and needed to be transferred to a state mental hospital.

Camera moves into the picture of Mickey and Mallory on the front page of the newspaper.

PHOTO: *Dewight McClusky.*

> WAYNE
> (*voiceover*)

We talked with Dewight McClusky, chairman of the California State Prison Board, about this curious turn of events in the Mickey and Mallory case.

INT. MCCLUSKY'S OFFICE – DAY

Wayne's interviewing McClusky.

> WAYNE

Why are Mickey and Mallory being moved to an asylum? And who made the decision?

> MCCLUSKY

The prison board made the decision. A board to which I belong. We're the who. The why is simple. Mickey and Mallory are mentally ill and need to be under a doctor's care, where hopefully they'll receive the help they need.

> WAYNE

Mickey and Mallory were deemed competent in a mental examination before their trial. I'm confused, what's changed?

> MCCLUSKY

Well, since that time, they've killed one person during their trial. And since their incarceration, they've killed one psychologist along with several guards and inmates.

> WAYNE

When they were found competent before, they had already killed fifty people. Other than the fact they're a disciplinary problem, which frankly shouldn't surprise anyone, I still don't see where the situation is any different from what it was before. So, I ask you again, Mr McClusky, what's changed?

> MCCLUSKY

What's changed, Mr Gayle, is our minds. We felt they were competent a year ago. A year has passed, sir, a year where they were under close observation, day in and day out, and their behavior has led us to believe we were wrong.

WAYNE

Who is we?

MCCLUSKY

The prison board and the doctors who examined them.

WAYNE

Were any of the doctors who made the first evaluation on the Knoxes' mental state asked to re-examine them?

MCCLUSKY

Using the same doctors is not common practice.

WAYNE

I take it from your answer it was a whole new team?

MCCLUSKY

Now that you bring it up, yes. They were different men. I hadn't really thought that much about it. Since many psychiatric opinions are, as a rule, sought out for this kind of situation. What do you think normally happens? The Knoxes are assigned a family psychologist who takes care of them throughout the rest of their lives? The state doesn't work like that.

PHOTO: *Dr Albert Rodriguez*

WAYNE
(*voiceover*)

The two psychiatric opinions the board sought were those of Albert Rodriguez . . .

PHOTO: *Dr Felix Vargus*

. . . and Dr Felix Vargus. Both of the good doctors, for whatever reason, refused to be interviewed.

INT. DR REINGHOLD'S OFFICE – DAY

Back with Dr Reinghold. He's laughing.

DR REINGHOLD

It's a funny situation, actually. If anyone besides Mickey and
Mallory gave a damn, what the prison board is doing would be
considered an outrage. The prison board is basically saying, 'We
can't handle these guys.' They've moved 'em around twice since
their sentence started. They were a handful everywhere they
went. Now the prisons they're at now want them outta there. But
no other prison's gonna be stupid enough to take 'em. So the
prison board is left scratching their heads wondering what they're
gonna do.

Well, what they decided to do was to set up a kangaroo medical
court that found them crazy. Then they get them transferred to
Nystrom Medical Asylum or Lobotomy Bay as it's referred to in
psychiatric circles. Put 'em on a strict dope and electric-shock
diet, and Mickey and Mallory cease to be a problem to anybody
except the orderlies who clean out the bedpans, which, if you want
to see them get theirs, is all well and good. But there's something
being said here. Forget the immorality for a second. Forget the
corruption and the skulduggery involved. What the board is
saying is, 'We give up.' Mickey and Mallory ran amok in polite
society. They were put in an alternative society and they ran amok
there, too. All the powers that be can't deal with these two kids.
And whatever can't be assimilated has to be terminated.

WAYNE

So, in your opinion Mickey and Mallory are not insane?

DR REINGHOLD

Insane, no. Psychotic, yes. A menace to living creatures, yes. But
to suggest that they're insane gives the impression that they don't
know right from wrong. Mickey and Mallory know the difference
between right and wrong. They just don't give a damn.

Freeze frame on Dr Reinghold.

INT. EDITING BAY – DAY

*Wayne's just finished viewing the show. He puts his hands on Scott's and
Roger's shoulders.*

WAYNE

Good work, my brothers. Fan-fuckin'-tastic! I think that
interview stuff's too long, we can lose some of that. Keep the girls,
keep the long-hairs, keep the Hun brothers, keep the black guy,
keep the movie shit, and keep the cop at the donut shop. Lose the
rest. And cut the interview with the prison board fellow before
that. Cut it after I ask, 'I take it by your answer it was a whole new
team.' Don't even let him answer. Fuck him. Then cut to me
talking about the two chicken-shit psychiatrists and straight into
Dr Reinghold laughing.

SCOTT

OK.

Wayne puts his arm around Unruly Julie.

WAYNE

Children, we have a show.
                    (*to Scott and Roger*)
You two get some long, well overdue sleep. 'Cause tomorrow,
bright and early, county jail and then journey's end . . . Mickey
Knox.

CUT TO:

TITLE CARD:

'TOMORROW – BRIGHT AND EARLY'

INT. MICKEY'S CELL – DAY

Mickey's pacing back and forth in his cell, trying out different jokes.

MICKEY

There's this Italian guy, a French guy, and a Polish guy. And
they're all talkin' about how they fuck their wives –

JUMP CUT:

. . . You know, I'm gonna just rip off your dress and squeeze your
titties. Then Little Red Riding Hood whips out her .357, sticks it
in the Bag Bad Wolf's face and says, 'No you're not. You're gonna
eat me . . . just like the story says.'

66

JUMP CUT:

> *(with a lisp)*
>
> . . . Fairy boat! I knew things were good in here, but I didn't
> know we had our own Navy.

JUMP CUT:

> . . . So this guy wants to take little Johnny's sister to the drive-in.
> But the mother says, 'Only if you take little Johnny along – '

JUMP CUT:

> . . . And the Polish guy says, 'That's nothing. When I get through
> with my Hanna, I get up, wipe my dick on the curtain, and she
> hits the roof!'

JUMP CUT:

Mickey's pretending he's calming down a hysterical audience.

> No . . . please . . . thank you . . . you're too kind . . . no . . .
> please . . .

INT. NEWS VAN – MOVING – DAY

Through Scott's camera, we're filming this in black and white 16mm.

*Note: Every time we view through Scott's camera, we are filming
handheld in 16mm black and white. Unless otherwise specified, the shots
stay in Scott's camera.*

*Scott's filming the back of the news van. Roger's sitting in the back eating
donuts, as is Wayne. Unruly Julie's up front driving.*

> WAYNE
> *(with mouthful of donut)*
>
> How's it working, Scotty?

> SCOTT
> *(off)*
>
> Perfecto!

*Roger's picking through a box of donuts. Scott pans over to him, then
slowly zooms in on him.*

ROGER

Where the fuck's the chocolate cream-filled? Did anyone get my chocolate cream-filled? If you did, it's mine.

CU of Roger, looking into camera.

I pointed at a chocolate cream-filled. You saw me do it, didn't you?

Wayne starts talking. We pan from Roger to a CU of Wayne.

WAYNE

You were there. Did you see him put it in a box?

We pan back to CU of Roger.

ROGER

At the time, I was too busy explaining to Scott the finer points of film.

We zoom back to a wide shot.

SCOTT
(*off*)

Yeah, right. You know what he said? He said, *Indiana Jones and the Temple of Doom* is Spielberg's best film.

Wayne starts laughing. We hear Scott laugh, too.

WAYNE
(*to Roger*)

You can't be serious?

ROGER
(*preoccupied*)

I'm as serious about that as I am about going back to that donut store, and dipping that stupid Mexican's head into the batter for forgetting my chocolate cream-filled. Gimmie that other box.

WAYNE

Huh uh. This dozen is for Mickey.

ROGER

That dumb-ass probably put my chocolate cream-filled in there by mistake.

WAYNE

Roger, no.

ROGER

What's the big deal? Take out my chocolate cream-filled, put one of these roasted coconut –

WAYNE

Roger, do you understand what the word 'no' means? It's important we establish a rapport. Something as simple as a dozen donuts can mean the world to somebody who hasn't had a donut in a year.

ROGER

So you're giving a man who butchers whole families, little babies included, my chocolate cream-filled?

Unruly Julie honks the horn. Wayne gets up and looks out the windshield.

WAYNE

OK, guys, we're here. LA County Jail. Julie, just park in the front. Scott, come with me.

ROGER

Wayne –

WAYNE

Roger, I'm starting to get pissed. Just drop this fuckin' donut shit, and gather your gear.

The van stops. Wayne slides open the panel door, and steps out.

EXT. LOS ANGELES COUNTY JAIL – DAY

We're back to color 35mm. Wayne hops out of the van and is approached by Superintendent Phil Wurlitzer, who's followed by two Deputy Sheriffs.

WAYNE
(*aside to Scott*)

Here's the welcome wagon.

Wurlitzer reaches them and shakes Wayne's hand.

WURLITZER

Hello, Mr Gayle. I'm Phil Wurlitzer. We talked on the phone. It's a pleasure to meet you.

WAYNE

Same here. Let me introduce my crew. Scott . . . Roger . . . and Unruly Julie . . . this is . . . I'm sorry. What's your title again?

WURLITZER

I'm the superintendent here at LA County Jail. Me and my deputies are who you'll be working with while you're here.

WAYNE

That sounds great. Look, I don't want any of this to intimidate you. This is not going to be a big deal. This is going to be very easy.
(to his crew)
I need to talk with Mr Wurlitzer. You guys just get all your equipment ready. Julie, help 'em.

Wayne speaks confidentially to Wurlitzer as they walk toward the entrance.

The main thing I need is a big room, shut off from the population, so we can get some privacy . . . with a few electrical outlets.

INT. SUPPLY ROOM – DAY

Wayne and his crew have set up in the food supply room off from the cafeteria. Being big, roomy, and unpopulated, it's perfect for an interview. There are eight LA County Deputy Sheriffs around the room along with Wurlitzer. Roger's setting up his sound equipment while Unruly Julie is checking her notebook.

Wurlitzer and a few Deputies talk among themselves. Camera moves from person to person without cutting.

WURLITZER
(to two Deputies)
This is just right for an interview. I was on the set of *Dukes of Hazzard* once. It was a much bigger deal than this. They had a crew of maybe seventy-five people.

Camera moves to Wayne and Scott.

> **WAYNE**
>
> We're gonna be talking over here. But I want enough freedom so if I wanna get up and move around, we can.

Wayne grabs Scott and walks him to the left.

> Take him and walk him over this way.
> *(pretending Scott is Mickey)*
> So, Mickey, killing Mallory's parents, what the hell was that all about?
> *(pause – to Scott)*
> Then maybe take him to the window.

He walks Scott to the window.

> *(pretending Scott is Mickey)*
> So, Mickey, if you were let outta jail today, what's the first thing you'd do?
> *(pause – to Scott)*
> Little shit like that. I don't wanna have to feel I gotta stay in the chairs. We're after a *cinéma-vérité*, anything can happen, truth twenty-four times a second kinda feel.

End of single shot.

Wurlitzer's talking with Deputies.

> **WURLITZER**
>
> And when it's lunchtime, they don't just go to McDonald's. They got cooks there servin' great food. Swedish meatballs . . .

Wayne walks over to Wurlitzer and Deputies.

> How's everything coming, Mr Gayle?

> **WAYNE**
>
> Everything's coming along just fine. Phil, I wanted to know if I could have a small word with you.

> **WURLITZER**
>
> By all means.

Wayne puts his hand on Wurlitzer's shoulder. They walk around the room.

71

WAYNE

You met the kids I have working for me? Great bunch, aren't they?

WURLITZER

Oh yes, indeed. Top flight.

WAYNE

Scott, genius cameraman. Roger, magician with sound. Unruly Julie, I would sooner do without my arm than Unruly Julie.

WURLITZER

Is that her real name?

WAYNE

Just a little nickname. Yep, they're my kids and they're all I need. After working together these past coupla years, we're like well-oiled machinery. No, more like a formula race car. No, scratch that one, too. What we're really like is a Swiss watch. Small, intricate, compact . . . it shouldn't work as well as it does, but it does. Because of the craftsmanship, the expertise, and the artist's loving hand.

Wayne gives Wurlitzer a moment to digest this.

WURLITZER

I see.

WAYNE

Now, Phil, I don't know if you've ever been on a set before –

WURLITZER
(*proudly*)

Ya know, I was.

WAYNE
(*acting surprised*)

Really?

WURLITZER

I was on the *Dukes of Hazzard* set about eight years ago.

WAYNE
(*still acting surprised*)

Well . . . small world. Well, then, you know firsthand how

Hollywood does things. Lights all over the place, generators, a hundred and fifty crew members –

WURLITZER
Oh, that *Dukes of Hazzard* show, there was probably ninety-five people there, maybe more.

WAYNE
See what I mean? It's a funny business, isn't it?

WURLITZER
It sure is.

WAYNE
They got a asshole over here.
(*pointing to his left*)
A asshole sitting down reading a magazine over there.
(*points to his right*)
A asshole perched up there.
(*points straight up*)
Assholes everywhere. Hey, maybe if we were doin' that kiss, kiss, bang, bang stuff we'd need all those assholes, too. What we're about is intimacy. We're about two people having a conversation. Say I was interviewing you. All I want you to worry about is what I ask you. I want a trust to develop. If you're thinking about all this . . .
(*indicates the hustle and bustle of a set*)
. . . you're not going to relax, a trust won't devleop. We'll be talking at each other instead of to each other, there will be no chance for intimacy.

Wayne gives Wurlitzer a chance to take this in.

That's why my crew is only three . . . an invisible three.
(*switching gears*)
Which brings me to what I wanted to talk to you about. I have to get Mickey Knox to relax . . . Mickey Knox to share what he's never shared before . . . Mickey Knox to open doors which till today have been closed. Well, how can we expect him to do that when we got Los Angeles County Deputy Sheriffs up the ass?

Suddenly, things get short between the two men.

73

WURLITZER
(*snorts*)
Well, just what the hell do you expect me to do?

WAYNE
Lose 'em.

WURLITZER
Mr Gayle, do you have the slightest idea how dangerous Knox is?

WAYNE
Mr Wurlitzer, I assure you, I am very familiar with Mickey
Knox's career.

Now they're out-and-out angry.

WURLITZER
Since he and his wife have been in custody, they've killed –

WAYNE
Don't recite the facts to me. I'm sure I know 'em better than you
do.

WURLITZER
Well, let me let you in on one fact you obviously don't know. If I
were to take my men away, Mickey Knox would snap your neck
like a twig.

WAYNE
One . . . I can take care of myself. I grew up in a tough
neighborhood, and I've handled some pretty rough customers in
my day. Mickey Knox doesn't scare me. Two . . . I'm a journalist,
and I'm prepared to take that risk. Three . . . it ain't gonna
happen. Believe me when I tell you, it is in Mickey Knox's own
best interest to play this game according to Hoyle.
(*pause*)
Wait a minute. We've gotten into an adversarial relationship here,
which is not what I want.
(*pause*)
But seriously, Phil, look at this.

Wayne scans the room, counting the Deputy Sheriffs.

74

(*counting*)

We got one . . . two . . . three . . . four . . . five . . . six . . . seven . . . eight. I mean, Jesus Christ, Phil, that's too much. Let's lose some of these guys.

WURLITZER

Wayne, if it was anybody else –

WAYNE

Phil, I'm just scared he's gonna clam up on me with all these sheriffs all over the place. They hate him. He hates them. What kinda intimacy am I gonna create with all this hate in the air. Even you and I feel it.

WURLITZER

What are we talking about?

WAYNE

Two guys?

WURLITZER

OK. I'll take two guys off.

WAYNE

No, no, no, no, no, no, I mean only two guys.

WURLITZER

I can't do that. Five guys.

WAYNE

Three.

WURLITZER

I'll cut it in half. Four guys, but that's it.

INT. MICKEY'S CELL – DAY

Two Deputy Sheriffs swing open the door to Mickey's cell. Mickey's lying on his bed with his hands behind his head. The two Deputies are carrying the chains and the belt.

DEPUTY #1

Get on your feet, turn your face to the wall.

Mickey gets up.

MICKEY

Now what you're supposed to say is, 'Five minutes, Mr Knox.'

CUT TO:

INT. SUPPLY ROOM – DAY

Shot through Scott's camera:

Camera pans from Wayne standing at the window to the door as two Deputies lead Mickey into the supply room. From time to time, another Deputy or Wurlitzer or Wayne will come into frame, but we're just following Mickey.

WURLITZER
(off)

OK, boys, let's start undoing him.

The two Deputies start unlocking the chains. As they do, Mickey looks off screen at Wayne.

MICKEY
(to Wayne)

OK now, before we get started here, there's a few things we have to get clear about.

WAYNE
(off)

OK, Mickey.

MICKEY

Let's discuss it when I'm unbound.

Camera holds on Mickey standing still as the two Deputies remove the chains.

INT. MALLORY'S CELL . . . DAY

CU of Mallory asleep in her bunk. We hear the sound of the cell door being opened. Mallory wakes with a jolt. She springs out of bed, crouching into a fighting stance.

SCAGNETTI
(*off*)
Rise and shine, Mallory! Beautiful day for a drive, isn't it?

INT. JAIL CORRIDOR – DAY

Mallory's bare feet walking in front of two Deputies' shiny black shoes. The deputies are Bingham and Washington.

The sound of Mallory's bare feet slapping against the concrete floor along with the clip, clop, clip, clop of the Deputies' hard shoes reverberating through the scene.

Mallory walks slightly ahead of the two shotgun-wielding Deputies. Scagnetti moves beside her. He lights up a cigarette with his Zippo lighter, and takes a long drag.

SCAGNETTI
It's a long trip to Bakersfield. Long and hot. Ever been to Bakersfield before?

Mallory looks straight ahead.

I've been there twice. And I'm not lookin' forward to goin' back. But I'm in and out. You, on the other hand, sweetheart, are gonna spend the rest of your life there. Now that's what I call cruel and inhuman punishment.

Mallory shows no emotion, just keeps on walking.

Course you're not gonna give a shit. 'Cause when the good doctors get through givin' you the zap . . .
  (*he puts his finger next to his temples, mimes being electrocuted*)
. . . You won't know where the hell you are. They'll just put you on a window-sill, and water you every other day.

Mallory lets out a big yawn.

INT. HOLDING CELL – DAY

Camera is inside a holding cell fixed on the cell door. The cell door is unlocked, then opened. The two Deputies bring Mallory inside. Scagnetti wanders in, trailing behind.

77

Bingham pumps his shotgun slide and places the barrel next to Mallory's head. Washington unlocks the cuffs around Mallory's wrists.

Mallory's silent.

Scagnetti leans up against the wall, smoking his cigarette.

> BINGHAM
Turn around and face the wall!

Mallory does.

Bingham and Washington move to the door.

> SCAGNETTI
Wait outside for a second, fellas.

> BINGHAM
We're not supposed –

> SCAGNETTI
Don't worry about it.

Bingham and Washington move outside.

Scagnetti takes out his gun and tosses it to Washington. Before they can protest, Scagnetti closes the door.

Mallory stands in the middle of the cell, motionless, her back to him.

Scagnetti walks up behind her.

Mallory doesn't move.

> SCAGNETTI
Want a smoke?

Mallory's steel eyes glare at Scagnetti.

C'mon, I already lit one for you. I know you smoke.

Mallory doesn't respond. Scagnetti takes the cigarette from his mouth and puts it between Mallory's lips. Hold on CU of Mallory.

> (off)
I was reading the file on you. You know what it said? It said during your trial, whenever they put you on the stand, no matter what they asked, your answer was always the same . . . 'I love

Mickey.' It also says that when they gave you a polygraph, 'I love Mickey' was the only thing you said that registered as the truth.

Scagnetti appears at the side of frame next to Mallory.

Who are you supposed to be? Squeaky Fromme? Is that it? Is Mickey your Charles Manson? Is Mickey Jesus? Is that the attraction? Or does he just got a big dick?

Scagnetti changes to Mallory's other ear.

That's it, isn't it? Mickey's got a big donkey dick.

Scagnetti presses closer.

Can you remember the last time you fucked? Huh? What I want you to do is close your eyes and remember . . . remember the last time ol' Mickey gave you the high hard one. Are ya thinkin' about it? Good. Remember it. Don't ever forget it 'cause it ain't never gonna happen again. 'Cause when they get through with all that electro-shock shit they got lined up for you two, Mick's dick ain't gonna be worth shit.

Mallory spits the lit cigarette into Scagnetti's face. Scagnetti spins her around and slaps her.

Look. You're gonna sit here for a couple hours while I finish up the arrangements. The reason they picked me to be your chaperon is they know I won't hesitate to put a bullet in you.

Scagnetti has Mallory clutched tightly by her shoulders.

So, during our journey, if any wild hairs spring up on your ass, you'd better slap a muzzle on 'em! Fuck with me, bitch, even a little bit, you're gonna get accidentally shot! *Comprende?*

Mallory looks at him for a moment, then gives him a massively hard head butt to the nose. As we hear the cracking sound of his nose, Scagnetti lets out a horrible scream.

EXT. HOLDING CELL – DAY

Bingham and Washington fumble with the keys to open the cell door.

INT. HOLDING CELL – DAY

Bingham and Washington burst through the door to find Scagnetti face down on the ground.

Mallory's standing, her foot pressed against the middle of Scagnetti's back, pulling his arms behind him trying to break his back. His body is bending like a branch, and he's screaming.

The two Deputies proceed to beat the shit out of her with their shotguns.

Scagnetti rolls around in the background, holding his bloody nose, screaming.

SCAGNETTI

She broke my fucking nose! That bitch broke my nose!

Washington comes over to him and helps him up.

(*blood down his face*)

She broke my nose.

WASHINGTON

I'll fix it.

He grabs Scagnetti's nose, then snaps it back into place. Scagnetti lets out another horrible scream, and hops up and down from the pain.

When the rush of pain passes, Scagnetti brings his hands down from his face, looking over at Mallory.

Bingham has Mallory in the corner of the cell with the shotgun barrel placed in her mouth.

CU on Scagnetti. He's a hand-grenade with the pin pulled.

SCAGNETTI

Hold her, boys.

Scagnetti walks to the corner where Mallory is. The shotgun barrel's out of her mouth. Bingham and Washington stand on either side of her, holding her in place.

Scagnetti grabs a can of mace from Washington's belt, and brings it up to Mallory's face.

Mallory and Scagnetti trade looks.

Scagnetti gives her an intense blast of mace right in the face, eyes, and all down her body.

Mallory crumples to the floor, screaming in agony.

Two-shot of Bingham and Washington looking down at Mallory on the ground. We can hear Scagnetti still spraying her. They can't look at this anymore.

Mallory wiggles on the floor as Scagnetti continues spraying her all over her body.

CU on Scagnetti's bloody, smiling face. We hear the sound of the can of mace running empty. It spurts to a stop.

Scagnetti rises up to the two Deputies. He hands the empty can back to Washington.

> SCAGNETTI
> I want you to get that filled again before we leave.

The three men walk out of the holding cell, closing and locking the door behind them. We can still hear Mallory's screams of excruciating pain.

INT. SUPPLY ROOM – DAY

Mickey's sitting in a chair eating a donut. Roger's attaching a microphone to his shirt. Unruly Julie's applying make-up to Mickey's face.

> MICKEY
> (*to Unruly Julie*)
> How come you never talk?

> ROGER
> She was born without a tongue.

> MICKEY
> (*repulsed*)
> Oh my God!
> (*to Unruly Julie*)
> Sorry.

Unruly Julie shrugs her shoulders like 'What ya gonna do?' and continues applying pancake.

Wayne and Wurlitzer talk.

> WAYNE

So we got a deal. Four deputies –

> WURLITZER

And me.

> WAYNE

Why don't we make it three deputies and you?

> WURLITZER

Why don't I have Mickey thrown back into his cell and we can forget the whole thing?

> WAYNE

Chill out, Phil. Four deputies and you, I can live with that. We're about ready to go here, so let's get rid of these other assholes.

> WURLITZER

Don't call my men assholes.

> WAYNE

I didn't mean they were assholes. I mean if they're leaving, get 'em outta here.

Wayne leaves Wurlitzer and goes over to Scott, who's setting up a light stand.

OK, Scotty, we're stuck with four of these assholes. Now I want to create the illusion that this is just Mickey and I chewin' the fat all by ourselves. So make sure you don't film these assholes. I don't want to see 'em on film ever.

Wurlitzer's speaking with his four Deputies.

> WURLITZER

This asshole's tryin' to tell me what I'm gonna do in my jail. Fuck him! This nanderfuck doesn't know what he's dealin' with here, but we do. And if shit happens, he ain't gonna be responsible, we are. So keep your shotguns out, your fingers on the triggers, and be ready to fire at a moment's notice.

BACK TO:

Mickey alone in frame, sitting in a chair and eating a donut. He takes a big bite.

> ROGER
> (*off*)

Say something.

> MICKEY
> (*mouth full of donut*)

What?

> ROGER
> (*off*)

Anything.

Mickey swallows the bite of donut, pauses, then recites a poem.

> MICKEY
> (*talking in rhyme*)
> The house began to twitch,
> rising to a pitch.
> And then the hinges started
> to unhitch.
> Just then the witch,
> to satisfy an itch,
> was flying on her broomstick,
> thumbing for a hitch,
> and, ooohhh, what happened then
> was rich.

Roger joins him in frame and adjusts the mike. Mickey bites into the donut.

> (*mouth full of donut*)

How was that?

> ROGER

Fine. Let me make an adjustment here, and we'll be ready to rock 'n' roll. Oh, the dumb-ass at the donut place put a chocolate cream-filled I asked for in your box.

> MICKEY

There's a chocolate cream-filled in there?

                                ROGER
Yeah. Ya see, I ordered that special.

                                MICKEY
Tough titty, it's mine now.

                                ROGER
Look, I'll trade you. I'll go back to the van and get –

Wayne enters frame.

                                WAYNE
Roger, enough with the fucking donuts! Stop bothering Mickey,
and get back behind your nagra.

                                ROGER
                            (*to himself*)
Fine. Roger, what the hell are you doing? You're bothering the
serial killer.

Roger exits frame.

Wayne grabs a chair and sets it in front of Mickey.

                                WAYNE
Sorry about that.

                                MICKEY
Don't worry about it.

                                WAYNE
We're about ready to go here. Are you ready?

                                MICKEY
Let's do it.

INT. SUPPLY ROOM – DAY (MINUTES LATER)

*Scene is now shot through Scott's camera. Camera will focus and follow
Mickey and Wayne, whatever they do.*

                                WAYNE
Tell us what you do for fun.

84

MICKEY

Aside from the obvious?

Mickey breaks out laughing.

WAYNE
(*not amused*)

Yes. Aside from the obvious.

Mickey's laughing slowly runs its course.

MICKEY

OK, let me see now. What do I do for fun?
(*to people off*)
Does anybody got a smoke? You guys are drivin' me crazy with
your cigarettes.
(*to camera*)
Sorry out there in TV-land. I'm just sitting' here lookin' at these
Deputies smokin' up a storm, and it's really doin' it to me.

*A Deputy comes into frame, hands Mickey a cigarette, then lights it.
Deputy exits frame.*

Much obliged. What do I do for fun? Do you want to know what I
do for fun or what I did for fun?

WAYNE

What? Oh, aaahh, what you did for fun for starters.

MICKEY

What I did for fun for starters.
(*thinking*)
Well, something I use to do . . . always was a lot of fun . . .
(*pause*)
No, scratch that. Let me think of something else. In fact, why
don't we come back to that question. Ask me something else.

WAYNE

Do you miss Mallory?

MICKEY

Of course, I miss Mallory. She's my wife. I haven't seen her in a
long time. What a stupid question.

WAYNE

Then was it worth it?

MICKEY

Was what worth it?

WAYNE

Was massacring all those people worth being separated from your
wife for the rest of your life?

Mickey takes a drag on his cigarette.

MICKEY

Do you think up these questions or the girl with no tongue?

WAYNE

No, Mickey, I can't let you get away with that shit. Answer the
question. Was it worth it? You haven't seen, heard, or smelled
Mallory in a year. Was it worth it?

MICKEY

Was an instant of purity worth a lifetime lie? Yeah, it was.

WAYNE

Excuse me, did you say an instant of purity? What was the instant
of purity? The bodies you left behind on your bloody trail?

MICKEY

That's only part of it. I mean, it's a big, big, big part. But it's only
the chorus, it's not the whole song.

WAYNE
(*passionately*)

Please explain to me, Mickey, where's the purity that you couldn't
live without in five-year-old Danny Hillhouse's blown-off head?
Where's the purity in forty-eight people who are no longer on this
planet because they met you and Mallory? What's so fucking pure
about that?

*Camera zooms in on Mickey's face. Mickey looks at Wayne, takes a slow
drag on his cigarette.*

MICKEY

Where the purity comes into play –

86

Black leader fills the screen.

SCOTT
(off)

We've run out.

WAYNE
(off)

Fucking dammit! Mickey hold on to that thought. Change it quick.

Moments later, we're looking through Scott's camera again on a new reel of film.

You just said an instant of purity was preferable to a lifetime lie. I don't understand. What's so pure about forty-eight dead bodies?

MICKEY

You'll never understand. Me and you, Wayne, we're not even the same species. I used to be you . . . then I evolved. From where you're standing, you're a man. From where I'm standing, you're an ape. I'm here . . . I'm right here . . . and you . . . you're somewhere else, man. You say why? I say why not?

WAYNE

Tell me about the purity.

MICKEY
(laughing)

It's not that easy, Wayne. Donuts and a smoke only get you so far. You're gonna have to do your job.

WAYNE
(laughs)

OK . . . OK . . . I'll buy that. We'll move on and come back later.

MICKEY

I'm sure we will.

WAYNE

Describe Mallory.

MICKEY

Describe Mallory? OK. She's pretty, she's got blond hair, two eyes, two feet, two hands, ten fingers . . .

87

WAYNE

Don't play dumb with me, Mickey. You know what I mean.
Describe Mallory.

(*points at his head*)

What's up here?

(*points at his heart*)

What's in here?

MICKEY

That's indescribable.

WAYNE

Well, riddle me this, Batman. How do you feel about the fact that
you're never gonna see Mallory again?

MICKEY
(*smiles*)

Says who?

WAYNE

Says the United States of America.

MICKEY
(*laughs*)

When have they ever been right?

The crew laughs off screen.

(*laughs*)

Hey, just like Soupy Sales.

INT. HOLDING CELL – DAY

We're back to color 35mm.

*Mallory's on the ground, splashing water on her face from the holding cell
toilet. The pain has started to subside.*

All wet, she lies down on the ground and sings:

MALLORY
(*singing*)

Love is a hurtin' thang,
and it leaves a fiery sting.

88

INT. JAIL CORRIDOR – DAY

Scagnetti walks down the hallway leading to the supply room. His nose is covered with medical tape.

INT. SUPPLY ROOM – DAY

Scagnetti walks into the supply room. Mickey is explaining to Wayne why he killed all those people. Scagnetti can't believe what he's seeing. The entire room is in rapture.

> MICKEY
> . . . one night I'm asleep, and a noise wakes me up. I think, 'Oh shit, somebody's broken in.' I don't own a gun, so I go into the living room with a fucking umbrella. OK, it turned out to be nothing, God made the noise. Who knows?

> SCAGNETTI
> (*whispers*)
> How's it goin'?

> WURLITZER
> Shhh! I wanna hear this.

Wurlitzer sees Scagnetti's bandaged face.

> What the hell happened to you?

> SCAGNETTI
> You should see the girl.

Camera leaves them and travels the room, studying the faces of the Deputies, Unruly Julie, Roger, and Wayne as they listen to Mickey's story.

> MICKEY
> But I came to the decision I needed a gun. So, the next day I started off early for work, and I was gonna stop by a gun shop and pick up a little home protection. I walked into the place and had never seen so many guns in all my life. So, I'm lookin' around, then this really nice sales guy comes up to me. His name was Warren. I'll never forget his name. He was really nice.
> Anyway, Warren showed me all these different models of guns.

Magnums, automatics, pistols, Walters. And I ask to see a
shotgun. He brings me a Mossberg pump-action shotgun. As soon
as I held that baby in my hands, I knew what I was gonna do. It
felt so good. It felt like it was a part of me. They had a mirror in
the store. I looked at myself holding it, and looked so fuckin'
good, I immediately bought it. Bought a bunch of boxes of ammo.
Turned my car around, drove to Mallory's house, we took care of
Mallory's parents, packed up the car, and we were off.

Shot through Scott's camera.

Medium CU – Mickey.

Everybody thought I'd gone crazy. The cops, my mom,
everybody. But you see, they all missed the point of the story. I
wasn't crazy. But when I was holding the shotgun, it all became
clear. I realized for the first time my one true calling in life. I'm a
natural born killer.

> WAYNE
>
> OK, let's cut it.

BACK TO: *Color 35mm.*

> *(to Scott)*
>
> Did ya get that?

> SCOTT
>
> It's gonna be beautiful.

> WAYNE
>
> Super cool.
> *(to Mickey)*
> This is great stuff. How ya doin'?

> MICKEY
>
> I could go for a Coke.

> WAYNE
> *(yelling)*
> Could I get a Coke for Mickey?

> WURLITZER
>
> I'm not running out and getting that piece of shit a Coke.

90

WAYNE

Fine, be that way.
(to Unruly Julie)
Julie, why don't you make a food run?
(to the room)
What's around here?

DEPUTY SHERRIF

There's an In and Out Burgers about a block away on Olive. It's walking distance.

WAYNE

OK, Julie, take everybody's order. I'll have a double double with cheese, french fries, and a large Coke.

Unruly Julie writes down Wayne's order in her notebook, then goes from person to person collecting their orders.

Scagnetti and Wurlitzer talk to each other.

WURLITZER

Are you all set?

SCAGNETTI

Yeah. Bus is all gassed up and ready to roll.

WURLITZER

I assigned you Bingham and Washington to go along.

In background, Unruly Julie takes Scott's and Roger's orders.

SCAGNETTI

Yeah, we met. They're good men.

WURLITZER

They're real goddamn good. They'll be there for ya when ya need 'em. Where are they?

SCAGNETTI

Waitin' in the lounge.

WURLITZER

How 'bout Mallory?

Coolin' her jets in a holding cell.

Unruly Julie walks up to the two men to take their order. In the background, we hear the wall phone buzz.

Nothing for me. I'm leavin'.

WURLITZER

Me, neither. I don't eat meat.

Unruly Julie walks away. A Deputy yells for Wurlitzer.

DEPUTY SHERRIF

Capt'n!

WURLITZER

Yeah!

The Deputy holds the receiver of the wall phone in his hand.

DEPUTY SHERRIF

They need you. Emergency!

Wurlitzer rushes to the phone, grabs the receiver.

WURLITZER
(*into phone*)

Talk to me.

(*pause*)

Where?

(*pause*)

For the love of Pete . . . OK . . . OK . . . OK. Mobilize the men.
I'm on my way.

Camera pans away from Wurlitzer to the extremely curious eavesdroppers.

Camera glides by all of them: Scagnetti, Wayne, Scott, Roger, Unruly Julie, and finally ends up on Mickey.

Off: the sound of a telephone receiver being slammed down.

WURLITZER
(*off*)

I'll be a son of a bitch. There's a riot going on in the laundry room.

> DEPUTY SHERRIF
> (*off*)

Is it serious?

> WURLITZER
> (*off*)

It sure as hell is. They got guns, hostages, and explosives.

The room reacts.

Jack, could you stay up here for a while?

> SCAGNETTI
> (*off*)

Yeah, sure.

> WURLITZER
> (*off*)

I'm taking one of these men. Yates, come with me.

> WAYNE

Could we go with you and film it?

> WURLITZER
> (*off*)

Stay up here and finish your interview. I've got to see what the hell's going on down there before I can take responsibility for you to film there.

We hear Wurlitzer and Deputy Yates walk out.

Unruly Julie walks into frame next to Mickey. She has her notebook.

> MICKEY

I'll have a four by four. That's four patty burgers. Now they don't have that on the menu, but if you order a four by four, they'll know what you're talking about. A large Coke and two orders of fries.

When she finishes writing down Mickey's order, camera follows her out the door as she leaves.

INT. JAIL CORRIDOR – DAY

We dolly with Unruly Julie as she walks down the corridor, while Deputies with shotguns and riot gear speed down the hall.

INT. SUPPLY ROOM – DAY

Shot through Scott's camera:

Focus on Mickey, who's standing in a medium shot.

> MICKEY
>
> You guys wanna hear a joke I heard?

> WAYNE
> (*off*)
>
> Sure.

> MICKEY
>
> Now, I'm no comedian, but it's pretty funny. It's a Little Johnny joke. Now in the joke, Little Johnny can't talk. And Little Johnny's teenage sister asks her mother if she can go out on a date.

As Mickey tells this joke, he moves around the room. Scott's camera follows.

> The mother asks, 'Where's he taking you?' The sister says, 'The drive-in movie.' The mother tells her she can only go if she takes Little Johnny with her. She says OK. They go to the drive-in, they come back. The mother gets Little Johnny and says, 'OK, what happened? Where did ya go?'

Mickey, as Little Johnny, draws a square in the air, and acts like he's driving.

> Mother says, 'The drive-in movie. What did they do?'

Mickey, as Little Johnny, acts like he's kissing.

> 'They kissed. What else?'

Mickey, as Little Johnny, starts squeezing imaginary breasts.

> (*surprised*)
> 'He felt her up? What else?'

Mickey, as Little Johnny, acts like he's undressing.

> (*dumbfounded*)
> 'They took off their clothes? What else?'

Mickey, as Little Johnny, acts like he's giving a blow job?

'She sucked his thing? What else?'

Mickey, as Little Johnny, vigorously acts as if he's having sex.

'They did it? What were you doing?'

Mickey, as Little Johnny, vigorously acts as if he's jacking off.

Everybody in the room breaks up. Wayne, the Boys, the Deputies, even Scagnetti cracks a smile.

As Mickey was telling the joke, he stopped in front of Deputy #4 during the punchline.

While everybody's laughing, Mickey slams his elbow in Deputy #4's face. Mickey grabs hold of the shotgun, rips it from Deputy #4's grasp, then bashes him in the face three times with the butt.

Deputy #4 drops, ugly and unconscious.

Scott's camera goes wild.

BACK TO: *Color 35mm.*

The other Deputies react.

Mickey pumps the shotgun slide and shoots, killing Deputy #1 and hitting Deputy #2 in the chest, blowing him off his feet. He lands on his back with a thud.

Deputy #3 raises his shotgun. Mickey drops to a crouching position and fires, blasting Deputy #3 in the groin. Deputy #3 crumples into the wall, firing his gun – slow motion.

The stray bullet thunks Scott right in the chest, blowing him out of frame.

Deputy #3 drops to the floor, firing his shotgun straight up – slow motion.

CU – ceiling being blasted. Chunks of plaster and rock rain down on Deputy #3.

Scagnetti has whipped out his gun and is bringing it up to fire – slow motion.

Mickey, still crouched down, spins around toward Scagnetti – slow motion.

*Scagnetti has his gun aimed at Mickey. Squatting, Mickey has the
shotgun trained on Scagnetti. They're positioned across from each other on
opposite sides of the room.*

Nobody fires.

*We dolly past the faces of both Wayne and Roger, who are flat on the
ground, scared to death.*

CU – Scagnetti's face.

CU – Mickey's face.

*CU – Scagnetti's finger putting pressure on the trigger, then camera moves
up to a CU profile of his face.*

*Overhead shot of Mickey. Camera moves down in front of him into a CU
on his face.*

> MICKEY
> Looks like we got a Mexican stand-off.

> SCAGNETTI
> Slide the shotgun over here, put your hands behind your head,
> put your forehead on the floor.

> MICKEY
> Or what? You'll wound me? I can blow you in half and you know
> it.

> SCAGNETTI
> I've never wounded anything in my life. I got you locked right
> between the eyes.

Mickey rises.

> MICKEY
> If you don't drop that toy, I'm blowin' you in half on three. So, if
> you got me locked, take the shot. One . . .

Dolly in on Scagnetti's gun in foreground, past the gun, to his face.

CU – barrel of shotgun.

> (off)

> Two . . .

96

Dolly continues closing in on Scagnetti's face.

Wayne watches, wide-eyed.

Extreme CU – Mickey's face.

Three!

Medium shot on Scagnetti.

SCAGNETTI

Hold it! Don't shoot!

He clicks the hammer back into place on his gun, then points the gun up.

MICKEY

Open the chamber. Empty the shells.

Scagnetti does. The shells fall out.

The shells fall on the floor at Scagnetti's feet – slow motion.

Toss it.

Scagnetti does.

Now put your hands behind your head.

Scagnetti does.

Mickey, holding the shotgun, walks up to Scagnetti. They stand, facing each other.

Did you ever see *Eldorado*?

SCAGNETTI

What?

Mickey clouts him across the face with the shotgun. Scagnetti hits the ground, once again holding his bloody nose and screaming his head off.

Mickey looks at Wayne and Roger on the ground.

MICKEY

You guys stay on your bellies.

ROGER

Yes, sir.

Mickey bends over Scagnetti and takes hold of his right hand.

> MICKEY
>
> I am the most dangerous man in the world.

Mickey snaps the trigger finger on Scagnetti's right hand.

Scagnetti screams.

> And when the most dangerous man in the world tells you to do something, you oughtta think twice before refusing.

Mickey snaps the trigger finger on Scagnetti's left hand.

Scagnetti screams.

Mickey's still bent over Scagnetti.

> (*points at Scagnetti*)
>
> You're the law.
>
> (*points at himself*)
>
> I'm the law breaker.

Scagnetti's not going to give Mickey any more trouble.

Mickey stands straight, looks toward Wayne and Roger.

> Donut, get your camera. See if it's broke.

> WAYNE
>
> Let me check on Scott. He's hurt bad.

> MICKEY
>
> Scott's dead. And unless you wanna play follow the leader, shut up and do as you're told.

Roger's checking the camera. He turns on the motor. It's running.

> How is it?

> ROGER
>
> It's running.

> MICKEY
>
> OK, Wayne, your little movie just underwent a title change. It's now called *The Escape of Mickey and Mallory*. Starring me, you, Mallory, and special guest accomplice, Jack-fucked-up-fingers-

Scagnetti. Donut, get ready to roll. I want this for posterity.

Shot through Scott's camera:

OK, donut, I want you to move in for a close-up.

Camera zooms into a CU of Scagnetti.

>   (*off*)
> OK, buddy boy, where ya keepin' Mallory? I know she's still
> here, and I know you know where. So, start talking or my first
> work as a director will be your death scene.

>   SCAGNETTI
>   (*slightly out of it*)
> She's in a holding cell.

>   MICKEY
>   (*off*)
> You're taking us to that holding cell. Cut.

The camera shuts off.

CUT TO BLACK.

Moments later, camera is rolling again.

*Wide shot of Mickey, holding his shotgun. He walks over and grabs the
shotgun from dead Deputy #2. Deputy #2 won't let go of the gun from
his dead man's grip. Mickey finally yanks it loose. He extracts all the
shells from the gun, picks them off the floor, and puts them in his pocket.*

Mickey picks up Scagnetti's gun and slips it into his pants.

>   MICKEY
> OK, Jack, this is what we're doing. Stand behind me, put your
> back against mine.

Scagnetti rises, insecurely. He presses his back against Mickey's.

> Now if I feel your back move away from mine, you're gonna be
> ripped apart. Got it?

Scagnetti's back to back with Mickey.

>   SCAGNETTI
> Yeah.

99

MICKEY

OK, Wayne, step forward.

Wayne enters frame. Mickey extends the shotgun.

Keep comin'. Put your solar plexus against the barrel.

Wayne does.

Either one of you two move, it's gonna be shotgun city. You understand?

WAYNE/SCAGNETTI

Yes.

MICKEY

You ready, donut?

ROGER
(*off*)

Yes.

MICKEY

Wagons, hooaaa!

The hostage train starts moving. Wayne's walking backwards with the shotgun barrel pressed against his stomach. Mickey's walking forward, holding the shotgun. Scagnetti's walking back to back with Mickey as a shield.

Roger follows, filming them.

INT. HOLDING CELL – DAY

BACK TO: *Color 35mm.*

Mallory's sitting Indian-style, singing Girl Scout songs to herself, and doing the hand motions.

MALLORY
(*singing*)

Whataleeatcha, whataleeatcha
dodaleedo, dodaleedo.
Whataleeatcha, whataleeatcha
dodaleedo, dodaleedo. Simplest thing

there isn't much to it.
All ya gotta do is dodaleedo it. I
like the rest,
but the part I like best is
Whataleeatcha, whataleeatcha dodaleedo,
dodaleedo, do
quack, quack.

*The cell door opens and the hostage train of Wayne, Mickey, Scagnetti,
Roger and the camera, and two Deputies they picked up along the way
enters the room.*

CU – Mallory. She can't believe her eyes.

> MICKEY
> (*to Mallory*)

Honey, I'm home.

*Mallory runs into Mickey's arms, passionately kissing. This kiss has been
a year coming. Now they're doing something everybody told them they
would never do again.*

*For this moment they are the only two people on earth. We are
enraptured, too. Camera does a 360 around the loving couple.*

> MALLORY
> (*in between kisses*)

It's taken you so long to come to me.

INT. JAIL LAUNDRY ROOM – DAY

*This scene is a traveling CU of Wurlitzer. Although we'll only see
Wurlitzer, we can make out activity in the edges of the frame and we can
vividly hear the sounds of chaos around us.*

> WURLITZER

I want two men stationed in that tier, and I want men with rifles
all along the walkway.

> PITNEY
> (*off*)

Capt'n!

Wurlitzer walks over to a table and looks down.

Here's the layout of the laundry room.

WURLITZER

Where do the air ducts lead into?

PITNEY
(*off*)

Here.

SMITHY
(*off*)

Problem is they'll hear somebody approaching that way.

PITNEY
(*off*)

We turned off the power when they took over the room.

WURLITZER

We turn it back on and the machines go back to supplying us with the cover noise we need. Smithy, do it.

SMITHY
(*off*)

Right away, Capt'n.

Camera follows Wurlitzer as he heads in another direction.

WURLITZER

Jonesy, are the sharpshooters in place?

JONESY
(*off*)

Yes.

WURLITZER

You sure?

JONESY
(*off*)

I think –

WURLITZER

Never say you think when you know, or you know when you think.

Wurlitzer snatches a walkie-talkie.

>(*into walkie-talkie*)
Bergman, you in place?

>BERGMAN
>(*off – from walkie-talkie*)
Sure am, Capt'n. Nothin' clean yet.

>WURLITZER
>(*into walkie-talkie*)
Pass this to your team . . . the second they get a lock on a blue, they're to take the shot. Do you understand?

>BERGMAN
>(*voice from walkie-talkie*)
That's a big ten-four, Capt'n.

Wurlitzer looks to his right.

>WURLITZER
What do you think, Pitney? How much explosives do you think they really have in there?

>PITNEY
>(*off*)
It's hard to say, Capt'n.

>WURLITZER
Take a wild stab!

>PITNEY
>(*off*)
I'll say enough to destroy the jail.

>WURLITZER
The entire jail?

>PITNEY
>(*off*)
That's my opinion.

>BAILEY
>(*off*)
Here's the list of the rioters.

Wurlitzer takes it. He reads, then looks up.

WURLITZER
Wait a minute, Bailey. Where's the list of the hostages?

BAILEY
(off)
I'm working on it, Capt'n.

WURLITZER
Keep on it, son.

Wurlitzer reads the list to himself as he paces.

(reading the names)
Alvarado, Issacs, Julian, Martinez, Newendyke, Olvera, Pool,
Ramos, Schmidt, Spivey, Walsh, Westerguard . . .

Wurlitzer drops into a chair, exhausted. He rubs his face with his hands.

NAPALATONI
(off)
Capt'n.

Wurlitzer looks up, then looks back down.

WURLITZER
What is it, Napalatoni?

NAPALATONI
(off)
Mickey Knox is loose.

Wurlitzer looks up.

WURLITZER
What do you mean he's loose?

NAPALATONI
(off)
He's armed, he's killed three deputy sheriffs and one of Wayne
Gayle's guys. At the moment, he's holed up with Mallory Knox in
her holding cell with Wayne Gayle, another TV guy, that cop
fella, and two more deputies he picked up as hostages on the way
to her cell. What'd ya wanna do, Capt'n?

Wurlitzer holds a frozen look.

INT. HOLDING CELL – DAY

Shot through Scott's camera:

Camera is sitting with the other hostages. Mickey and Mallory stand above them, holding their weapons.

                              ROGER
                              (*off*)
We're rolling.

                              MICKEY
OK, we're going out that door, and we're gonna march down the
hall and right out of the building.
                              (*to Wayne*)
Donut said something about a news van.

                              WAYNE
Yeah, we have a van.

                              MICKEY
Where's it parked?

                              WAYNE
Out front.

                              MICKEY
Let me have the keys.

Wayne hands the keys to Mickey.

                              WAYNE
Mickey, can I talk to you alone?

                              MICKEY
No.

                              WAYNE
This is crazy. You can't escape like this.

                              MICKEY
Probably not, but we're gonna give it the old college try.

                              WAYNE
We'll all be killed.

MALLORY

Exciting, isn't it?

MICKEY

Now, when we get out there, you do what we say or it's curtains. If we say move, you move. If we say left, you move left. If we say right, you move right. If we say mole, you dig a hole. Got it?

MALLORY

Are we in a big hurry?

MICKEY

You got something you want to finish?

MALLORY

Yeah.

MICKEY

By all means, knock yourself out.

MALLORY

Thanks.

Mallory points to Scagnetti sitting on the floor.

You! Stand up!

Scagnetti gulps, then rises, knowing that he fucked with the wrong woman.

Mallory walks up to him, pistol in hand.

You probably thought it was pretty funny, didn't ya?

She raises Scagnetti's pistol, aiming it at its former owner. Scagnetti flinches and squirms.

Can you remember the last time you fucked with me? Close your eyes and remember . . . Are ya thinking about it? Good.

Mallory fires three shots into Scagnetti's chest. Roger's camera follows the body to the floor and holds.

CUT TO BLACK.

We hear over the black:

MICKEY
(*off*)
We're sending out a hostage. Don't touch him!

INT. OUTSIDE OF HOLDING CELL – DAY

Roger rolls film again, filming with Scott's camera. Camera moves out of the cell.

There are even more Deputy Sheriffs now.

Mickey and Mallory emerge from the holding cell, blasting with their guns while using the hostages for shields.

The Deputies fire back.

One of the hostage Deputies is shot, and discarded by Mickey.

The wild caravan runs down the hallway, Mickey and Mallory fire behind them.

Mickey's hit, but keeps on running and firing. Mallory sees this and screams.

MALLORY
Mickey!

MICKEY
Don't stop!

Roger and camera run along with them, filming.

ROGER
(*off*)
Man, oh, man . . . this is better than Vietnam!

This footage is very similar to Vietnam footage. It's shaky, real, harsh, and it captures the pandemonium of battle.

The soundtrack is a mad mixture of yelling, crying, laughing, and gunfire.

More Deputies appear at the end of the hallway.

Mickey and Mallory get back to back with each other, using a hostage as a shield in front of them. Mickey fires from the front, Mallory fires from the rear.

Roger's hit, and the camera goes haywire, reeling out of control, then thunking to the ground. Roger screams off screen.

Camera lies on the floor, film still rolling.

> MICKEY/MALLORY
> (*off*)
> Get the camera! Get the fucking camera!

BACK TO: *Color 35mm.*

As Mickey fires cover for her, Mallory swipes the camera from Roger's dead hands.

The Knoxes start running again, still holding Wayne and one last hostage.

Deputies are lying on the ground, wounded and screaming, or dead and silent.

> MICKEY
> (*to Mallory*)
> This way.

INT. STAIRWELL – DAY

The caravan enters a stairwell. Mickey turns to Duncan Homolka, the remaining hostage Deputy.

> MICKEY
> (*to Duncan*)
> Where does this lead?

> DUNCAN
> To the ground floor.

> MALLORY
> Is that the front door?

> DUNCAN
> Yeah.

> MICKEY
> Let's go.

The caravan starts running down the stairs.

As they run down one last flight, they find Wurlitzer and a team of Deputies waiting for them on the ground floor. The Deputies raise their guns.

Mallory grabs hold of Wayne, and gets behind him with one hand pressing the barrel of her gun against his temple and her other arm wrapped around his neck, holding him close to her.

MALLORY
Back off or I'll blast him! Back off or I'll blast him! Back off or I'll blast him!

None of the Deputies lower their guns, but they appear less likely to start shooting.

Wayne has tears streaming from his eyes. He screams:

WAYNE
Don't shoot! I beg you, don't shoot! Please, please, please . . .

Wayne continues begging.

Wurlitzer steps forward.

WURLITZER
Now Mickey, Mallory, just let me say –

MALLORY
Shut up! Don't talk, I don't wanna hear it!

WURLITZER
You have to know –

MALLORY
I said shut up . . .

Mallory quickly lowers her gun from Wayne's head and shoots him in the thigh. She whips the gun back up to his head.

Wayne's screaming in pain.

The Deputies jump back.

. . . and I mean shut up!

There's a silent stand-off.

The caravan slowly retreats back up the stairs to the next flight.

The Deputies hold their present position.

CUT TO:

INT. PRISON STAIRWELL – DAY

The caravan goes up one flight, then stops. Mickey and Mallory let their two hostages sit down.

Mickey's pacing around.

> MICKEY
> Think . . . think . . . think . . .

Mallory leans up against the wall, holding her side with her hand. Blood trickles out between her fingers. We now see she's been shot.

They can hear Wurlitzer yelling from below to 'Give up! There's no way out!' etc.

Mickey sits down, utterly exhausted. Mallory sits down next to him. She winces in pain. He puts his arm around her.

> MALLORY
> Look, lover boy, we're not getting outta here. So, I say the hell with going back to our cells. Let's do a Butch Cassidy and the Sundance Kid. Run down these stairs shootin', go out in a hail of bullets, but take as many of those motherfuckers with us as possible.

Suddenly, Mickey's exhaustion lifts. He has a plan.

> MICKEY
> We'll do that when all else fails.

> MALLORY
> Hasn't it?

> MICKEY
> We still got a few tricks up our sleeves.

Mickey stands up in front of the two hostages. He looks at Duncan.

> You married?

DUNCAN

Yes.

MICKEY

Got kids?

DUNCAN

Yes.

MICKEY

Good. People, we're goin' all the way to the front door. Now, the only way we're gonna get there is if they don't want to kill you two more than they want to kill us.

Insert: shots of Deputies with guns in their hands, just itching to kill Mickey and Mallory. We hear Mickey's voice over this shot.

(*voiceover*)

Right now I find that highly unlikely. So, let's help 'em out, shall we?

BACK TO: *The Knoxes and the hostages.*

Now, say I tell those guys down there if they shoot or make a move, I'm killin' Wayne Gayle, and they shoot or make a move anyway. Now say by some freak accident, you didn't die. You lived through it. What would you do?

WAYNE

What would I do? Me and my network would sue the entire Los Angeles County Sheriffs Department for flagrantly disregarding my safety. I'd go straight to my buddy, the mayor, and make sure every one of those sons of bitches down there ends up on the unemployment line. In fact, I'd sue every man down there personally. I would make it my life's ambition to bring the LA County Jail to its knees. I would do exposé after exposé on the brutality, and the conditions, and the inhumanity that exists here.

MICKEY

That's what I thought. You tell them that. When we go down those stairs, I want you to scream what you just told me. 'My name is Wayne Gayle! I am the star of *American Maniacs* watched every week by' – how many people?

WAYNE

On average forty million.

MICKEY

'– every week by forty million people. I am a respected journalist.'
Have you won any awards?

WAYNE

Are you kidding? The Golden Globe, The Edward R. Murrow
award . . .

MICKEY

'– respected journalist, winner of the Golden Globe and the
Edward R. Murrow award among others.' Tell 'em the name of
your personal lawyer, his firm, his address, and phone number.
Tell 'em about the mayor and the unemployment lines. You
getting the idea?

WAYNE

Yes.

MICKEY

Say it. Scream it. All the way out the front door and into your van.
And if you stop screaming, I swear to God, I'll blow your head off.

WAYNE

Got it.

Mickey grabs the camera, then sticks it in Wayne's hands.

MICKEY

Take this and point it right at them deputies. So if anyone does get
an itchy trigger finger, we got 'em on film, and they know we got
'em.

Mickey moves to Duncan.

You! What's your name?

DUNCAN

Duncan Homolka.

CUT TO:

INT. PRISON STAIRWELL – GROUND FLOOR – DAY

Wurlitzer and the Deputies are deciding their next move when they hear:

MICKEY
(*off*)

Start.

Wayne and Duncan come into view with the Knoxes behind them.

The Deputies quickly raise their guns.

Wayne and Duncan start yelling. Wayne aims the camera at the sheriffs.

WAYNE	DUNCAN
(*yelling*)	(*yelling*)
My name is Wayne Gayle! I'm the star of *American Maniacs*, watched by forty million people every week! I'm a respected journalist, winner of the Golden Globe award, the Edward R. Murrow award among others! If anybody puts me in danger, my network will sue the Los Angeles County Sheriffs Department. My estate will sue personally every officer who fires. The network's law firm is Rowlands, Davis, and Sinclair . . .	I'm Duncan Homolka, and I don't want to die! I've been on the force six years, and I don't want to die! My wife's name is Jamie, and I don't want to die! I've got two kids, Ben and Allison! Ben's six and Allison's seven, and I don't want to die!

Mickey knows what he's doing. This has an effect on the Deputies.

MALLORY
(*yelling*)

Make a path!

The wall of Deputies starts moving backward.

The Knoxes and their hostages start moving forwards with Wayne and Duncan yelling all the way.

All the Deputies keep their guns trained on the caravan, but they also keep moving backwards.

> WURLITZER

How far do you think you're gonna get?

> MICKEY

Right out the front door.

> WURLITZER

That'll never happen.

> MICKEY

It is happening.

Wayne and Duncan keep shouting their speeches. Nobody dares make a move on them, but the Deputies keep their weapons ready.

Duncan stops his speech.

> MICKEY/MALLORY

Don't stop!

Duncan starts up again.

Wurlitzer and the Deputies are completely frustrated.

> WURLITZER
> (*to Mickey*)

I will personally blow the head off your fucking whore, and plant your sick ass in the ground all by myself.

> MICKEY
> (*calmly*)

Another day perhaps, but not today.

Freeze frame: As Mickey and Mallory start firing, à la Butch and Sundance. We hear the gunfire and screams of a small war.

FADE TO BLACK

EXT. WOODS – DAY

CU – Wayne, filmed by a 16mm camera.

Both Mickey and Mallory are being interviewed and filmed by Wayne.

The entire scene is played out cinéma-vérité. *The sound is not in sync.*

> WAYNE
> (*to camera*)

This is Wayne Gayle. I'm wounded and my crew, Roger and
Scott, are dead. This may be out of sync 'cause we are recording it
with a standard tape recorder we found in the van. Mickey Knox's
plan worked. We shot our way out the front door into my news
van and made our getaway. When we were followed by patrol
cars, Mallory Knox killed Deputy Sheriff Duncan Homolka and
tossed his body out the back. Mickey told authorities over my
police band that I would surely be next if they didn't give up the
pursuit. They took Mickey at his word and called off the pursuit.
Why helicopters weren't employed, I don't know. My only
thought is it all happened too fast for arrangements to be made.
We've just pulled off to the side of the road to do this interview.
Tensions are running high –

Mickey screams off screen.

> MICKEY
> (*off*)

We ain't got all fuckin' day!

> WAYNE

Without any further ado, Mickey and Mallory . . .

*Wayne positions the camera so it's now on Mallory. Mickey, shotgun in
hand, paces back and forth tensely in the background.*

> (*off*)

Mallory, what did you think of Mickey's plan? Did you think it
would work?

> MALLORY

It wasn't till we got on the ground floor that I totally realized they
weren't gonna shoot unless we shot first. When we got out of the
stairwell, I remember thinking, 'Oh my God. This might just
work.' But Mickey knew it would work all along. There wasn't
any doubt in his mind. It's not like there was and he just didn't
show it. He knew it would work.

(*off*)

What did you think then?

MALLORY

I wondered how long it would be before we'd get to be alone
together. And I wondered if I could wait that long.

WAYNE
(*off*)

Did you have anything to do with the riot in the laundry room?

MALLORY

Haven't you been listening to a fuckin' word I said? . . . Oh, I'm
sorry. Can I say fuckin'? I can't, can I?

WAYNE
(*off*)

Try to keep it to a minimum.

MALLORY

We had nothing to do with that riot . . . That riot was just –
whatchmacallit . . .

MICKEY

Divine intervention.

MALLORY

What he said. We didn't know jack shit about any riot. It just
happened. It was kismet. We didn't even know those people. How
are we supposed to organize a riot when we've been in fuckin'
isolation for the past year? Just bleep out the fucks and jack shits.

Mallory starts laughing.

I mean, it's not like we care. If they wanna say we masterminded
the whole thing, let 'em. It won't exactly keep us up at night. But
you said you wanted the truth, and the truth is we were just lucky.

Mickey's snapping his fingers in the background.

MICKEY

C'mon, c'mon, let's hurry this up.

                                      WAYNE
                                       (off)
So, what now?

                                     MALLORY
Well, now me and Mickey are gonna take it easy. Just enjoy each
other's company, stop and smell the roses, notice the color purple,
stuff like that.

                                      WAYNE
                                       (off)
How do you intend to disappear? You're probably the most
famous couple in America.

                                     MALLORY
Well, back in slave times they had a thing called the underground
railroad. And we got a whole fan club out there just waiting to be
conductors.
                                  (to the camera)
So, you kids out there, keep the faith. Cause Mickey and Mallory
will be comin' to your town real soon.

                                     MICKEY
OK, that's enough. End of interview. We gotta move.

                                      WAYNE
                                       (off)
OK, just let me swing around and film myself asking the
questions. And then I'll do my little wrap-up.

                                     MICKEY
Oh, we're gonna do a little wrap-up, all right. But it won't be you
starin' in the camera, looking dumb, and acting stupid. Instead,
you're gonna be starin' down the barrels of our shotguns and we're
gonna be pullin' the triggers.

Wayne forces a chuckle.

                                      WAYNE
That's a joke, right?

*Mickey pumps the slide on his shotgun. Mallory grabs her shotgun from
off the ground.*

                                        117

WAYNE

Just wait one fucking minute.

MICKEY

I said I'd give you a interview. Now unless I'm mistaken, we just
did a interview.

(*to Mallory*)

We did a interview, didn't we?

MALLORY

Looked like a interview to me.

MICKEY

I said I'd give you a interview. I never said I wouldn't kill you.

WAYNE
(*off*)

Wait! I don't know, but I kinda felt during this whole escape that
a kind of bond developed between the three of us. We're kinda in
this together, don'tcha think?

MICKEY

Not really.

WAYNE
(*off*)

Don't touch those triggers! I think I've already proven that a live
Wayne Gayle is much more useful than a dead Wayne Gayle. I was
your passport out of jail, not those deputies. But me! I'll be your
passport outta –

MICKEY

Just save your breath, Wayne. We hate you. If anybody in the
fuckin' world's gonna die, it's gonna be you.

WAYNE
(*off*)

Wait a minute. You can't kill me. Mickey and Mallory always
leave somebody alive to tell the tale of Mickey and Mallory.

MICKEY

We are.

(*points in camera*)

118

Your camera.

Mickey takes the camera from Wayne and puts it on a rock, then he turns to Mallory.

Camera views the following:

> MICKEY
> (*John Wayne voice*)

Let's make a little music, Colorada.

The two interview subjects start pumping rounds into Wayne.

Wayne buys the farm.

Mickey and Mallory kiss each other, climb into the news van, and drive away.

Camera eventually rolls out of film.

CUT TO BLACK